the **SOUND ON SOUND** book of

recording & production techniques

for the **recording** musician

Design: David Houghton

Printed by: Staples of Rochester, Kent

Published by: Sanctuary Publishing Limited, The Colonnades,
82 Bishops Bridge Road, London W2 6BB

While the publishers have made every reasonable effort to trace the copyright owners for any or all of the photographs in this book, there may be some omissions of credits for which we apologise.

ISBN: 1-86074-188-6

Contents

introduction

A great deal of mystery surrounds the art of the professional record producer and studio engineer, for it is now recognised that their contribution to a record can be equal to that of the artist. Indeed, some producers have assumed a Svengali-like role, taking command of all stages of a project, from songwriting to final mix. In such cases, it has been known for the artist to make only a minor musical contribution; examples of this are rare and come to our attention only because of the publicity they attract, but they serve to demonstrate the enormous influence that can be exercised by the producer. However, the vast majority of producers work closely with the recording engineer and artist, the sole aim being the production of a commercially viable record.

The backgrounds and experiences of producers vary widely: some producers are competent engineers, while others come from a musical background and rely solely on the studio engineer to interpret their needs. As you will discover, it is the diversity of backgrounds and approaches that makes record production such a lively and involving subject.

The aim of this book is to explain the role of the producer and his relationship with the artist, recording engineer and record company. But I won't be neglecting the engineering side of things, and will also be covering the techniques that can be used to create specific sounds and musical effects. Equally valuable, you'll find information on liaising with clients and planning sessions; all aspects of a session are covered — from setting up to the final mix.

After the chapters devoted to the mix, you'll find a section addressing the little-understood area of post-production, which includes album compilation, audio sweetening, remixing and editing, as well as the final steps in producing a professional recorded product.

The recording and engineering techniques discussed in this book will be of benefit to the commercial studio engineer and potential record producer as well as the home recordist. In addition to the author's own experience, much of the information has been distilled from long conversations with top producers and engineers worldwide and is applicable to a wide range of musical styles and disciplines.

chapter 1

a little history

When you consider the flamboyant personalities and rock 'n' roll lifestyles associated with the music business over the past two or three decades, it might come as quite a surprise to learn that in the early days of recording, the whole process was very formal and, by modern standards, very basic. The first records ever made were recorded in mono, with very simple mixing techniques used to record what was, in effect, a live performance.

The only tools at the engineer's disposal in these early days were level faders; the first mixers had no EQ, so if the engineer wanted a different sound, he had to achieve it either by selecting a different mic or by changing the mic position. If a more ambient sound was needed, the only way of achieving this was to use a 'live' room; consequently, many improvised techniques, such as using reverberant concrete stairwells to add reverb to a mix, were pioneered during this period .

It was also commonplace for studios to build dedicated echo rooms in their basements. These were essentially large reflective rooms with angled surfaces, often tiled. A loudspeaker and microphone would be set up in the room, then any sound needing treatment would be fed into the room. The signal picked up by the mic would be added back into the mix, in much the same way as we add digital effects using the effects return channels on a multitrack console.

Company Men

In these early days, engineers and producers were full-time employees of the record company which also owned the studio. Because of this arrangement, the same people would work on a wide range of musical styles, covering classical, jazz, pop, ballads and so forth — which is why many of the 'old-school' engineers and producers are so versatile. In those days, efficiency was the prime objective, and because of the live way of working, whole albums were regularly completed in a single four-hour session; the Beatles' album *Please Please Me*, for example, was recorded in one 13-hour day! Engineers — wearing white lab coats — remained on one side of the control room glass, with the artists on the other. Rarely, if ever, was an artist allowed into the control room during a session!

What we now call record production was then split between two people; the musical director and the producer. This is a close parallel to the way in which things are still done in the film industry — the producer looking after the business side, and the director concentrating on artistic considerations. The musical director would be responsible for the musical arrangements, the quality of the musical performance and the sound and mix of the final recording. In turn, he would be under pressure from the producer to work quickly while spending as little money as possible! In the days when all non-pop backing music was provided by orchestras, a little wasted time could add up to a lot of money, and even today this is an area of concern. One major consideration is that orchestras tend not to be booked by the minute but in blocks of half an hour or so, depending on which country you are working in and the rules of the particular union to which the musicians belong. This means that 'just one more' take can take you into the next block of time, which can add hundreds or even thousands of pounds to the cost of a session.

Low-Tech

Technology improved to allow stereo recording, and this was soon followed by 4-track recording, which allowed singers to overdub their parts rather than tying up a live band or orchestra for every take. Basic EQ and pan pots were added to the mixing consoles, and the plate reverb was developed to eliminate the need for a live room. It was with this fairly basic technology that many of the classic pop records of the sixties were made, though many of the early Phil Spector-produced hits were recorded in mono. During this decade, the only real effects unit was the tape echo, though guitar amps were being built with integral electronic tremolo and spring reverb.

Around this time, improvisation was a vital ingredient to achieving a distinctive commercial sound and with no hi-tech processing to help, this involved a lot of experimentation. Rooms with interesting acoustics were pressed into service, while double-tracking was taken to extremes by some producers, who would hire in several guitar players, for example, to play identical parts.

When flanging was first discovered, it had to be created manually by recording the same piece of music onto two tape recorders, which would then be started at the same time. By using slight hand pressure on the tape reels of first one and then the other machine, the sync between the two machines could be made to drift in and out, giving rise to the characteristic whooshing sound used on so many psychedelic records. At the time, this effect could only be added after the recording; there was no way to achieve it live.

Changing Roles

The role of producer and musical director gradually merged, and if a producer lacked the specialised musical knowledge to arrange songs, he would hire in an arranger when required. Even so, the producer was still very much tied to his record company, and the relationship between George Martin and the Beatles was probably the greatest incentive to challenge the status quo. All the world knew just what an influence George Martin had on the Beatles and few doubt that he was a key figure in ensuring their continued success. This relationship inspired many producers to go freelance, which gave them the opportunity to negotiate royalties, or 'points', with the artist's management, at the same time allowing producers to specialise. Prior to this, the 'tied' producer had to make the best of any job that came his way, regardless of its musical style. And regardless of the commercial success of a record, the producer still only received his basic salary.

Things were changing, though, and it was also around this time that recording engineers were allowed to turn up for work without a tie! Rigidly-defined morning and afternoon recording sessions also became more flexible, with some musicians being allowed to record during the night. Musicians were even managing to get into the control room!

From this time the whole system became more flexible, with freelance studios springing up to accommodate the growing number of freelance projects. No longer was it set in stone that an artist had to record at his or her record company's studio with the company engineer and in-house producer. The more forward-thinking record companies recognised that certain projects could benefit from being handled by producers who favoured a certain musical style or who had a good track record in producing hit records. Inevitably these producers built up relationships with engineers they found it easy to work with, and so the freelance engineer was created. Now a musical act could benefit from working in the most appropriate studio with a sympathetic producer and an engineer who knew the producer's requirements.

This slackening of the old regime was a double-edged sword. On the positive side, it did allow the right people to work together and some great records were made, but in the late sixties and early seventies when the music business still made a lot of money, this freedom was frequently abused. Aside from the stories of all-night recording sessions consisting of sex, drugs and very little rock 'n' roll, work was seldom approached with any sense of economy. Bands would book studios for months on end and actually write the songs in there! Artist mismanagement was rife, and many young bands didn't realise that at the end of the day, it was their own money which was being wasted.

Advances

Much of this waste of resources and time was down to a basic misunderstanding of what a record company advance really is. It isn't just free spending money! When a company signs a band, they generally make available a sum of money for the band to live on and to enable them to go into the studio and make a record. All the studio expenses and any other cash advanced is ultimately deducted from the artists' royalties once the record starts to sell. If the record doesn't sell, then it's the record company, not the artist, who loses out — but in the past it was quite common for bands to have a hit single and then find that they received none of the proceeds from it because their share had all been frittered away in recording time, chauffeured cars and expensive catering. In other words, a record company advance should be considered as an unsecured, interest-free loan which is repaid when the artist's records begin to sell.

Over the past decade, the music business has suffered a considerable decline, partly because consumers now have interests other than collecting records and partly, so the record companies argue, because of unauthorised cassette copying. The truth probably goes deeper than that; the original sixties music generation are now middle-aged, with enough money to buy records but with little chance to hear any music that might appeal to them. It could be that the national obsession with the Top 40 has served only to alienate a great many potential record buyers; it is up to record companies and record producers to redress this situation.

chapter 2

the modern producer

Today's producer requires a significantly different range of skills to those of his sixties counterpart, though the underlying objectives of bringing in a commercially successful project at the right budget are still at the top of the list. Nowadays, the producer must have a flair for music (though he doesn't have to be a musician), he must have the right contacts, he must be able to plan finances and, not to be underestimated, it is essential that he be able to handle people.

Most producers come from a musical rather than an engineering background and have made their contacts during their years in the business. They will have worked in studios and, during that time, will have made contact with engineers, record company staff and other musicians who may be able to help out on future sessions. Current producers also tend to be familiar with MIDI, as much pre-production work is done using MIDI sequencing systems.

I have interviewed a great many of the top record producers over the past few years and nearly all have a different approach to the subject, so there's no absolute definition or job specification. Some are competent recording engineers, while others need a house engineer to do virtually everything for them. Some may only fine-tune the arrangements presented by the artists, while others may rewrite the whole thing and even replace band members with session musicians. The only bottom line is results and different producers have different ways of getting from A to B; the important thing is to get to B!

There is one point, however, on which most seem to agree and that is that the ability to handle people in a stressful environment is very near the top of the list of qualities which a producer needs. Working against the clock in an expensive recording studio can be very stressful, especially when things aren't going right, and the producer must shoulder the responsibility for ensuring that a creative atmosphere is maintained.

Musical Style

A great many record producers build a reputation for working in a particular style, but the more astute among them have realised that styles change, and if you allow yourself to get pigeon-holed, you run the risk of becoming out of fashion and hence out of work. Even so, it is only natural for producers to relate better to some styles of music than to others, and even the most broad-based producers tend to have pet areas in which they particularly like to work. The main thing is to appreciate the risks and take care to ensure you don't get left out in the cold when styles change, as they inevitably do. This may be a particularly apt warning in these times when dance music is so successful, but the production techniques are so different to traditional pop work that a dance-only producer might be hard-pushed to find work in any other area.

Project Planning

At one time, records were invariably made in the studio belonging to the record company with in-house engineering staff. In recent years however, alternative working methods have been developed, which have advantages both creatively and for the recording budget. After spending some time talking to the artists and their record company, a producer will, typically, listen to demos of their material and pick out the tracks that he thinks are most suitable for the album/single. This is done in consultation with the artist, but at the end of the day, the producer has the last word. Having said this, a lot depends on the band and on their track record and standing in the business — a top band with a proven chart track record will certainly have more say over which of their songs are chosen and how those songs are recorded. A new band, on the other hand, is likely to have rather less influence.

Even at this stage, it's important for the producer to develop a comfortable rapport with the artist. They will be working very closely together, and so it is essential to build a mutual trust and respect, otherwise friction can easily occur when the going gets tough. The emphasis is on teamwork, and the producer is there to function as team leader.

The Engineer

Recording engineers come from a variety of backgrounds, though most appear to have had some connection with music prior to getting into recording. Traditionally, the aspiring recording engineer started out in a commercial studio, making tea and maintaining the tape filing system while picking up what he could about recording from the resident engineer. He'd then work on a few pet projects during studio down time, help out on sessions and eventually, be in the right place at the right time to control a session of his own. Most of the tales I've been told include stories of ludicrously long working hours, poverty pay and an almost total lack of sleep. Even so, most successful producers have a 'right place at the right time' story and recognise this event as the turning point in their careers.

Over the years, I've answered countless enquiries from people who want to get into record production or studio engineering. Unfortunately, a lot more people want to do the job than there are vacancies available, and the old 'tea boy' entry into the business can no longer be relied upon. There are so many engineers around that studios can afford to demand some level of experience from would-be applicants; the trick is to gain experience without actually doing the job.

Recording Courses

Recording courses are available in several guises, from cheap and cheerful weekend introductory sessions run in budget studios to full-time courses at recognised educational establishments. There's no doubt that these courses can help to get you started, but they offer no guarantee of a job. Likewise, you can run a home studio and learn a great deal about recording that way, but this still doesn't guarantee you the job of your dreams. However, all experience is useful, and if it makes you better equipped than the next candidate, then it's worth it.

But being able to physically do the job is only the first prerequisite — you also need the right attitude. Engineering can be a very stressful job and, like the record producer, you have to be able to work with often highly-strung musicians in a confined, potentially stressful environment for long periods. You have to be able to think on your feet and anticipate problems, and you have to accept that nobody is going to suggest you take a tea break, let alone half an hour off for something so trivial as a meal! If anything goes wrong in a studio, it's always the engineer's fault (justified or not) so you need to be broad shouldered as well as possessed of infinite stamina.

An engineer doesn't have to be a record producer, but even so, a good engineer will anticipate a producer's demands so that when the producer wants to try out a little vocal compression or reverb, the engineer already has them patched in with suitable settings. Some producers are really not deserving of the title and the bulk of the creative work then falls to the engineer. However, in these cases, the engineer seldom receives any credit for his input — it's still the producer's name which ends up on the record sleeve.

Why Do It?

You might well ask why anyone becomes a recording engineer, because the work is arduous, not at all well paid and very often demands that you work anti-social hours — both in the number of hours worked and the time of night you eventually get to finish work. I can't even pretend to answer the question, but there seems to be an endless stream of people just waiting to take their place in that smoke-filled sweat-box that is the working recording studio control room. I've done a lot of engineering over the past decade and a half, but I've never been in the position of having to do it full time, all the time, so I've grown to enjoy it. If you're determined to be a recording engineer, then you'll get there in the end, but you have to be persistent — if you can't take banging your head against closed doors, you probably don't have the resilience for the job anyway.

chapter 3

planning a session

The planning for a recording project starts as soon as the artists meet the producer. In some circumstances, the artists themselves will be in a position to choose which producer they work with, but it is more often the case that the record company chooses the producer because of his or her track record with certain musical styles. Establishing a rapport with the artists is the first step towards establishing confidence, as is an exploration of the artists' own ideas as to how their material should be handled.

Some acts readily accept that they need the guidance of an experienced producer, but as musicians tend to be pretty self-opinionated types, it is also possible that they will resent the imposition of a third party who has the final say over their material. A good producer will tackle this problem at once by exploring the artists' own ideas and only then suggesting possible changes, rather than taking a hard line by dictating the way he intends things to be.

Demo

As previously mentioned, most producers will first listen to the artists' own demos. Some producers like to copy the demo cassette to open reel tape and then edit the tape to form a more workable arrangement. The edited demos are then played back to the musicians before proceeding. Taking this pre-production procedure even further, some musician/producers might want to program their subsequent ideas for the final song into a sequencer and present various options to the artists.

An experienced producer might draw the attention of the artists to sections that don't work well and then elicit their ideas as to how the problem can be rectified. With any luck, they can be subtly coaxed until they draw the conclusions that the producer has already come to — it's much easier if the artists think the ideas have come from them, as they are less likely to resist them!

Session Players

A more sensitive issue arises when band members have to be supplemented or even replaced by session musicians. This has to be handled carefully to avoid damaging fragile egos, and it helps if the redundant band members can play at least some part in the recording. For example, the drummer who has been replaced by a drum machine might sit in on the rhythm programming and, in addition, may be asked to play a few live fills — it all depends on the producer and on his personal approach to the job.

Some producers may want to use MIDI sequencing extensively, in which case the preliminary programming will be done next, and the artists may play little part in this. Artists can easily feel insecure in such circumstances, so it helps to get them as involved as is practical and to solicit their approval when things are changed. Even getting the drummer to record some of his own drum sounds into a sampler can be enough — the secret is to make everyone feel involved.

The Budget

Once the preliminary ground has been covered, the next step depends on the producer's approach and on the available budget. It can be artistically fruitful to allow a band to experiment as they go along, but when it comes to bringing a project in on time and to budget, the producer with a positive plan is likely to be more successful. In any event, a producer with definite ideas can't afford to give too much leeway, as he will have a pretty good idea at this stage of how the finished product should sound.

There are producers who like to be more open-ended, but a sensible approach is to do any experimental work in a low-budget facility or home studio and then move into the more costly facility when all the uncertainties have been taken care of. If the majority of a project can be undertaken in a musician's home or programming suite, it can be completed at a much lower cost than a traditional studio recording.

SMPTE And Sequencing

Whether MIDI is being used or not, it helps to stripe the multitrack tape with SMPTE (Society of Motion Picture and Television Engineers) time code, in case sequenced parts have to be added later and to facilitate automated mixing. SMPTE code should be striped to the tape at the prevailing TV frame rate, which is 30fps (frames per second) in the USA and 25fps in Europe. The other frame rate of 24fps is used exclusively for film work, and so-called 'drop-frame' should be avoided unless the project specifies it.

Even if the majority of the musical parts are to be sequenced at the mixing stage, it helps to put a rough stereo mix of the sequenced backing onto tape; this will allow the artists to work on their overdubs without having to worry about loading sequences. Strangely enough, though the prevailing wisdom is that sequencing MIDI parts directly into the mix is the right way to go, a surprising number of professional producers still like to record their sequenced instruments to tape. When asked why, they tend to reply that they feel more comfortable having something concrete on tape rather than relying on the vagaries of software. Additionally, they may profess to like what analogue tape does to the sound. They might also comment that making a commitment at this stage saves procrastination later on, but providing the time code track stays intact, it is still possible to lock up the sequencer and change a sound or melody line right up to the final mix. Perhaps this approach gives the best of both worlds, in that the producer feels a commitment has been made, yet he or she still has the complete flexibility afforded by the sequencer should it be necessary to revert to the original sequence.

There's another very valid reason for recording sequenced parts onto tape, and that is that the available synths, drum machines and samplers might not have sufficient polyphony to cope with the entire performance in one take. In this instance, the sequence must be played through with some parts muted and the different sections recorded to tape in several passes. This might involve adding effects as the sounds go to tape, simply because several different instrumental or percussion sounds may have to share the same tape tracks.

Before leaving the subject of sequencing, it is the producer's responsibility to ensure that backup disks are made of any working material and that proper notes are kept to describe sounds, effects and so forth. The producer also has to decide whether to work with the available instruments or whether to hire in extra equipment.

Vocals

The best time to record vocals depends on which producer you ask! Some like to get the main vocal down as soon as the bare bones of the musical backing have been recorded; their justification for this is that it allows any further instrumentation to be fitted in around the vocal line.

In any event, it helps to get a guide vocal down first for the same reason — and it also helps the other players navigate their way through the song. Often the singer gives his or her best performance when recording the guide track because there is less pressure to get it dead right. A good producer will keep the guide vocal until the end of the session just in case.

In home recording, we tend to record a vocal part all the way through and then run through it again, dropping in any phrases that weren't up to scratch. Some professionals work in this way too, but they are more likely to record several complete takes on separate tracks, from which the producer will compile one good, composite vocal track. The best phrases will be bounced down onto a new track, and if the desk is fitted with mute automation, this process is very simple. If no mute automation is available, the different phrases must be 'brought up' manually, using either the channel mute buttons or the channel faders. Good notes are essential in order to keep track of the wanted phrases during this process.

Hardware

Though frivolous experimentation is a waste of time and money, it is well worth setting aside a little time to try out different mics and compressors as the vocalist warms up, to see which give the best result. There are certain esoteric models known for their good vocal sound but, as is often found to be the case, what works magic for one singer may be quite unsuitable for another.

It is common practice to apply a degree of compression to vocals as they are recorded; this helps to get a good working level onto tape and evens out the worst variations in level. Further compression can be used during the mix, as required. Proper attention should also be paid to giving the singer a workable foldback or monitor mix. Most singers work best with a reasonable amount of monitor reverb to help them pitch their notes. If a singer has problems working with enclosed headphones, try a semi-enclosed type or suggest that they work with one can on and one can off. Spill from the phones into the vocal mic is unlikely to be a problem except at very high monitoring levels or where a click track is involved.

Drums

If the session requires a lot of real drums, it may be most cost-effective to book some time in a studio which has a good live room, but may have fairly basic 16 or 24-track equipment. It is important to ensure that the tape machine is compatible with those available in the studios that may be used for other parts of the project.

Most pop music tends to make use of sequenced drum parts, often augmented by manual percussion, manual hi-hat and cymbal parts and the odd tom fill. This is an easy way to work because the basic drum rhythm is locked into the sequencer. On the other hand, if the session demands real drums all the way through, and some instruments are to be MIDI sequenced, then the drummer usually has to play to a click track generated by the sequencer. Top session drummers can do this effortlessly, but drummers used to setting the tempo rather than following it may take some time to adapt.

Tap Tempo

If a less rigid approach to timing is beneficial, it is possible to record the rhythm section 'live' and then use a tap-tempo facility to create a sequencer tempo map of the actual performance. This usually involves tapping a button in time with the original performance, and it helps to have at least two bars of extra count-in to get the tempo in sync. However, such an approach is rare in pop music and even very proficient drummers tend to make use of some sequenced rhythm parts, both for convenience and to produce a very exact tempo.

Sequencing the snare and bass drum parts avoids all the problems of snare rattle or toms booming whenever the bass drum is hit, yet if the player's own drums are sampled and then triggered by a sequencer, the end result can still be very authentic. As a rule, hi-hat and cymbal parts should be played live where a human feel is sought, though for dance music, which is more mechanical, totally sequenced drum parts invariably work better.

Drum Miking

Recording drums probably involves more decision making than any other aspect of the session, but other than a suitable room, all you need is a good basic desk and a selection of suitable drum mics. Rock drum sounds tend to be recorded with the emphasis on the close mics, with the overhead or ambient mics used to fill in the cymbals. The exception is where a very big, ambient drum sound is required, in which case a studio with a large live room is needed, with additional ambience mics placed at a distance from the kit.

Jazz drums tend to be recorded the other way around — the stereo mic pair providing the main contribution, and close mics used to fill out the sound and fine-tune the balance.

Guitar

Guitar parts may be DI'd using one of the available studio preamps or speaker simulators, though for heavy rock, the miked sound is still the preferred option. Ultimately there is no best way; it's all down to personal choice. In many instances, chordal and rhythm parts can be DI'd very satisfactorily, while lead solos might benefit from the interaction between the amplifier and the guitar, especially if feedback is used to prolong sustained notes. Once again, one can mic up either a large stack or a small combo. Both produce their own distinctive sound, though a large setup needs a large studio to produce the best results. A small valve combo such as a Fender Champ or low wattage Mesa Boogie can produce excellent results in a small project studio.

Different results can be achieved by varying mic position and by choosing either dynamic or capacitor microphones. If two guitar parts need to be separated in some way, recording one with a dynamic mic and the other with a capacitor mic can help. Further differences can be created by using humbucking or single-coil pickups or by the subtle application of effects such as chorus. Additionally, EQ can be used both on the amplifier and the mixing console to emphasise different parts of the sound spectrum, and of course, the two parts can be panned to different sides of the stereo image. If the resulting sound is still confused, the guitar parts themselves should be examined to see if they are too similar or too busy. Sometimes playing a chordal part in a more restrained and simple way or applying a little string damping solves the problem.

Acoustic Guitars

Acoustic guitars invariably sound better when miked up, regardless of how good the internal bug or pickup system may be. Important acoustic parts can be recorded in stereo, but where the guitar forms part of a complex arrangement, a mono recording may well give more stability. Because of the problems of sound leakage when working with acoustic instruments, acoustic guitars are invariably overdubbed individually, using closed headphones to prevent spill from the backing track.

If a song needs to start with several bars of solo acoustic guitar, but that guitar part must be recorded as an overdub, it is important that the correct number of count-in bars is provided, with a suitable click track or guide hi-hat part. If you ever have to pick up a project where this has not been done, it is possible to turn the tape over so that it plays backwards and then record extra beats at the introduction of the song to extend the count-in to a suitable length. A short, dry sound is best for this, otherwise the timing may appear to shift slightly when the sound is heard in reverse, as it will be once the tape is played back normally.

Psychology

Recording can be a stressful experience, and it is part of the producer's job to be aware of mood problems and to tackle them as they arise. Open discussion should be encouraged if it is not allowed to run on too long, and any individual who is clearly in a less than ideal mood can often be diverted by giving them something useful to do, such as looking after a fader level or supervising drop-in points.

The good producer will also recognise the point at which an artist has worked too long to be giving of their best and he'll change the order of work to give that person a break if at all possible. Perhaps the worst time is when someone is repeatedly incapable of getting their part right; insisting on a break at this point can often be far more productive than allowing the person to struggle on stubbornly. Positive encouragement is the key, because as soon as you start to criticise a musician, his or her confidence is likely to suffer and the final performance will be so much worse for it.

If you can afford the tape tracks to keep a previous take while allowing the performer to do another, the feeling of security this gives may enable the player to give a more relaxed performance. The use of drugs and the excessive use of alcohol should be discouraged because of their detrimental effect on musical ability.

Corrective Editing

In extreme cases of inability to perform, it may be possible to edit together several attempts to provide one good version. For example, a one-off good vocal chorus can be 'spun in' for each chorus, using a sampler or open reel stereo recorder, while several dreadful guitar solos can often be edited to produce one good one. Session players can sometimes be used to perform critical sections with greater precision than the original musicians, but if these sections are to be edited, great care has to be taken to match the sounds. Even if the same guitar and amplifier is used to play part of a solo, the sound can be quite different simply because of the players' individual techniques.

Once all the necessary parts are safely on tape, then it's time for the mix. However, unless time really is tight, this should be done on a different day so that it can be heard with fresh ears.

chapter 4

arranging

When presented with a song to arrange, the producer has to consider not only the musical construction of the piece, but also the way in which the various sounds fit together. Thus arrangement can be divided into three distinct areas:

◆ The order in which the various musical sections are presented (intro, verse, chorus, bridge, middle eight and so on).

◆ The musical lines and rhythms which make up each part.

◆ The sounds chosen to play these lines and rhythms.

The order in which a song is arranged is very important – commercial material tends to work to a fairly rigid formula in that a distinct intro is followed by between three and five minutes of music. The traditional, melodic pop song tends to have:

◆ An easily recognisable verse/chorus structure, usually with a middle eight (which, despite its name, doesn't need to be exactly eight bars long).

◆ One or two 'bridge' sections.

◆ An instrumental solo, though this is not invariably included.

The chorus will be repeated frequently, the song often fading out over a repeated chorus line. Though musical fashions change very quickly, this traditional song structure has proved to be one of life's survivors. However, the dance musical genre has managed very nicely by breaking all conventional rules of musical structure, but even so, it conforms to rules of its own regarding tempo, rhythms and, to a large extent, the types of sounds used.

Because of the ephemeral nature of the commercial music market, a song has to attract the interest of the listener very quickly, and once the intro is over, it usually pays to get to the chorus pretty quickly. This may be achieved by such devices as:

◆ Shortening the first verse.

◆ Using a modified version of the chorus as an intro.

◆ Coming straight in with the chorus after the intro.

Another useful device is to use only part of the chorus when it first occurs; this creates a sense of anticipation, helping to keep the listener interested. Indeed, the ability to create an atmosphere of anticipation is the hallmark of a good songwriter, and often the ends of verses or link sections will contain musical hooks which make the listener want to reach the chorus. What makes a good hook is less easy to quantify it could be anything from a brass riff or a drum fill to a vocal phrase or synthesizer line. The important thing is that it's catchy and easily identifiable. The verse must also contain a hook of some sort, but again this can be created by the clever use of melody, by repetition, or simply by the distinctive vocal character of the singer. If you're trying to create a track for the pop market, don't be above using something that sounds childish or musically immature – the majority of singles buyers are not noted for their appreciation of the finer points of musical construction, and if something sticks in their minds, they're more likely to want to buy it.

As with most successful musical formulae, dance music has diversified into a number of recognisable sub-styles such as rave, techno, acid jazz, ambient and so on, but as these are always evolving, the only way to become familiar with the sounds and structures being used is to listen to as many current examples as possible. Even though traditional arranging methods may seem to have been abandoned in favour of hypnotic repetition and relentless rhythms, the best examples are still arranged in such a way as to keep the listener's attention and some clever production tricks are frequently employed.

Though dance tracks may appear to have a very informal structure, and there may be little if any differentiation between the verse and chorus, sounds come into and out of the mix so as to create the elements of change, anticipation and energy necessary to keep the listener involved. The most successful dance records combine a strong rhythm with a series of musical hooks to make the result more compelling, and to help it stand out from the competition. These could be as simple as using non-standard hi-hat figures or a catchy bass line, or a selection of alternative percussion sounds added over the usual bass/snare/hi-hat back beat. The musical tempo of most such records is quite predictable and lies within fairly rigidly defined limits for each style, but on top of the straight four to the bar rhythm, it is possible to bring in other rhythmic patterns to make the whole more interesting. In this respect, there is no substitute for analysing existing music to find out exactly what makes it tick.

Most traditional style pop songs are fairly easy to analyse with not too much going on at any one time. If anything, American arrangements tend to be musically busier than British ones, but it is interesting to note that many of the instruments are kept very low in the mix, especially distorted guitars, with the vocal line mixed well up front.

★TIP

Don't overlook existing successful records if you're aiming to write commercial music – commercial simply means music that will make money, and to make money, music needs to have a wide appeal. While you shouldn't aim to copy another track, there is no substitute for analysing existing music to absorb song construction and arrangement tricks of the trade. This is particularly true of dance music, and if you want to to keep up to date, you need to visit the major clubs, because what appears on radio is either 'safe' music with broad appeal or several months old. Exceptions are specialised late night radio and TV programmes which sometimes manage to get beneath the 'pasteurised' exterior of chart music.

Independent records tend to take far less time to get into production than releases from major companies, which is why a lot of the most up-to-date dance music you hear in clubs comes from independent companies.

Instrumentation

It is tempting for the inexperienced record producer or musical arranger to have too many parts playing at the same time, which can easily make for a cluttered, confused mix.

At the heart of nearly every pop song is the rhythm section, which might take the form of traditional drums and bass or may be entirely synthesised using drum machines and synthesizers. Either way, the idea is to make the bass instrument and the underlying drum rhythm work together to establish the rhythm of the piece. The way in which this is done depends on the type of music you are working with – definite styles and rules exists for specific musical forms such as funk, reggae, dance and so on, which are quite evident after listening to a few records in the genre. Even though the approach of all these styles may be quite different, the bass and drums work together as a unit and not as independent entities.

◆ Guitars and vocals tend to occupy the mid ground in terms of the musical frequency spectrum, as do pad keyboard parts, so it is important to arrange these so that they don't conflict. This can be accomplished partly by the choice of guitar and keyboard sounds, and partly by the musical lines they play. Where several instruments are playing together and there is a danger of the sound becoming muddled, they can be separated to some degree by changing the basic sounds to make them thinner (removing some low mid using EQ), by emphasising different parts of the upper mid using subtle EQ boost and by panning. However, don't rely on panning to solve all your problems, as a mix still needs to sound good in mono. If the problem persists, re-examine the musical arrangement and question the role of each sound or musical line you've chosen. Every musical part should exist for a reason, and if you discover a part that has no reason to be there, then you're probably better off leaving it out.

◆ At the top of the spectrum come the bright synth sounds, cymbals, high percussion and so on, and these add detail and interest to a mix that might otherwise be bass and mid heavy. Bright sounds needn't be loud in order to provide the necessary musical punctuation, and if high synth lines or high percussion parts are planned, it may be prudent to examine any cymbal or hi-hat parts to avoid overcrowding.

◆ Pad keyboard parts can either be placed low in the mix or they may be filtered so as to occupy a narrower part of the audio spectrum.

◆ Synthesised sounds can be corrected at source, while organ sounds might be set up using the drawbars and then filtered by means of EQ. For example, it might be useful to roll off all frequencies below, say, 150Hz to thin out the sound which will help avoid potential muddiness in the vulnerable lower mid part of the spectrum.

◆ Riffs played by instruments such as brass don't usually present a problem, as they tend to be placed in strategic positions rather than being allowed to play all the way through; guitar riffs, however, are often allowed to continue below verses or choruses. Clean guitar sounds tend to be easier to integrate into a mix than heavily distorted sounds, hence the popularity of bright guitar riffs for underpinning soul music, and a bright chordal sound cuts through well in any mix without killing other sounds that occur at the same time.

Drum Sounds

Pop music currently favours tight, snappy bass drum sounds, while dance music uses very bass-heavy sounds, often synthesised, to create a relentless and powerful four to the bar rhythm. Pop snare drums are usually deep and crisp sounding, but there is a lot of scope for variation depending on the style of song. Some pop songs demand a brighter, more jazzy snare sound, while for others, more of a techno sound is appropriate.

Most dance rhythm sounds can be traced back to Roland's TR808 and TR909 drum machines, and because these are no longer in production, they change hands for inflated prices on the second hand market. However, sampler owners can find plenty of sample CDs and CD-ROMS featuring these sounds, and most successful exponents of the genre either blend sounds or add further processing to give their sounds some individuality. For example, a TR909 bass drum is a deep, dull, synthesized sound, but blending it with a sharper kick drum sample can produce a hybrid sound that has both depth and attack.

Dance snares tend to be light and bright, and take a back seat to the bass drum, which provides the driving rhythm. These snare parts often play simple rhythmic figures rather than simply beating out two to the bar and again, serious dance music composers tend to sample drum sounds from other records, which are then further treated with effects or layered with other drum sounds.

For those working without a sampler, it is possible to trigger a bass drum sound from a drum machine at the same time as a low-pitched burst of sound from a synthesizer to create a similar effect. Alternatively, the Simmons electronic kick drum sound is often emulated on modern drum machines and this makes an ideal basis for a dance rhythm track.

★TIP

EQ can also be used to change existing sounds by a surprising degree, and the useful trick of radically boosting the bass control while applying low mid cut at around 220Hz adds a lot of weight to the sound. The upper mid can be tuned to between 4 and 6kHz and boosted to produce a harder, better defined sound.

Pop hi-hats tend to be fairly natural and bright, but because of the dance influence permeating mainstream pop, some songs make use of the older analogue machine hi-hat sounds. The only rule is: There are no rules!

Suitable dance drum sounds, mainly TR-series in origin, are included on most modern drum machines and on sample CDs and CD-ROMs, so only the most dedicated purist needs to seek out the original vintage equipment. You can also create your own analogue drums sounds using an analogue synthesizer that includes a noise source as well as oscillators. Because of the lack of polyphony of most old analogue synths, the best option is to create the desired sounds one at a time, then sample them.

Analogue synths feature heavily in dance music, not only for their rich sound, but also for their ability to be controlled in real-time. This is particularly important where the artist wishes to create impromptu, manually controlled filter sweeps. A great many dance tracks take their bass sounds from Roland's TB303 Bass Line, a combined analogue bass synth and simple sequencer. These were pre-MIDI, so specialised companies have emerged which make their livings out of devising ways to make pre-MIDI equipment either MIDI compatible, or at least sync'able.

Short, aggressive filter sweep sounds, sometimes known as 'thips and blips', are frequently used to create additional rhythmic elements within a dance mix.

Once again, there are thousands of CD and CD-ROM analogue synth and bass sounds that can be loaded straight into a sampler, but you still have no way to create real-time filter sweeps under manual control. Though some digital synths and samplers allow their filters to be adjusted via MIDI controller data, the reality is that many of these glitch or change in audible steps when you try to make rapid changes. Patching the output via an external analogue filter or via an analogue synth with an audio input is probably the simplest way of adding authentic vintage filter sweeps to a modern instrument. Alternatively, several companies build MIDI-compatible, rack mount analogue synths with conventional control knobs handling the main parameters.

Rock Music

For rock music, kick drums tend to be recorded with plenty of slap and a little after-ring, while the snares are quite deep with a well-defined snare sound. Like the bass drums, the toms tend to be quite solid sounding with a little ring and a nice, sharp attack. The floor toms tend to be tuned fairly deep, and there may be several higher pitched toms, including smaller concert toms. Rock cymbal sounds tend to be quite natural, with a fair selection of clangy cymbal 'bell' sounds or earth-ride sounds. The hi-hats often have a fair amount of rattle but this fits in OK with the overall sound.

Heavy rock rarely makes use of electronic drum sounds, and most drum machines contain a selection of suitable sampled 'real' sounds. The most important thing is to listen to how a real rock drummer plays and program the part accordingly — while it is acceptable to use unnatural drum parts for dance music, rock requires a sense of authenticity.

Guitars

Guitar treatments are covered in some depth elsewhere in this book, but problems do arise when working with guitar bands because both guitar players often want to play all the time and they both want to play loud! If this is the case, return to the basic song and find out what it needs – not what the players' egos think they would like to give it. A problem often found with bands who play live on a regular basis, but have little studio experience, is over-busy guitar parts. The band will use a wall of sound to fill up their live sound, but in the studio, the result is invariably far too cluttered.

Guitars with single-coil pickups take up less space in a mix yet still cut through well, and that holds true for both clean and overdriven sounds. Strats and their clones are very popular for this reason. If two guitars, both using overdrive, need to play together, examine the musical lines to see they aren't both playing the same thing for no good reason. Space can be created by making rhythm parts more rhythmic rather than merely letting one chord sustain into the next, and it is often possible to reduce the amount of overdrive while recording, which will increase the amount of tonal light and shade present in the sound, even if it is compressed later. Indeed, overdrive is often used as a device to create sustain, and it may be that a far more appropriate sound can be achieved using much less overdrive combined with a generous helping of compression. The compressor attack time can also be increased to give more bite to individual notes, which can help if the guitar is playing a repetitive part.

★TIP

It has already been mentioned that miking the two guitars differently can help make them sound distinct, and that choosing one model with single-coil pickups and another with humbuckers also helps. Further to these methods, it is possible to use the desk EQ to emphasise the 'bite' of the sound differently for each of the guitars. Typically, the presence or edge of a guitar can be anywhere between 2kHz and 6kHz, and by choosing a different frequency for each guitar, then boosting this by a few dBs, the resulting sounds can be brought even further apart. Additionally, if one guitar part is clearly the lead with the other playing more of a supporting role, a compressor or gate used in ducking mode can be used to punch the second guitar down by just 2 or 3dB while the lead guitar is playing. This small change in level will make a dramatic difference to the clarity of the mix, and the fact that the second guitar swells back in when the lead guitar stops helps maintain the illusion of power and energy.

Effects can also be useful in making the sounds stand out from the mix. A very slow flange effect really lifts a sound without making it appear too processed, while a slap-back echo using a single delay set at 50mS or so also creates a punchy, immediate sound.

Listening to some of the early Rolling Stones albums gives some insight into how a clear, exciting mix can be created with two or more guitars playing most of the time. This is all the more impressive when you consider that the recording equipment available at the time was far less sophisticated than many of us have at home today. Most recording at that time was done on either 4- or 8-track, and the only effects available were tape delays, plate reverbs and fuzz boxes.

Reverb and Guitars

Reverb can be a problem when used with guitars, especially with dirty sounds, as it tends to make the sound sustain even longer; this fills up all the spaces that are so vital in allowing the mix to breathe. Short, bright reverbs work better in busy rock mixes, with longer settings being better suited to slow, melodic solos. Also try ambient reverb settings, and don't be afraid to use the reverb in mono (panned to the same position as the original sound), if you want to avoid the guitar sound becoming too spread out.

★TIP

Ducking can be brought into play to hold down the level of reverb in the mix until there is a break in the guitar playing, at which point it will swell back in to create the desired effect.

Ultimately, arranging music is an art, and with some modern genres, the dividing lines between composition, arranging and production have become almost non-existent. As with any art, you can benefit a lot from looking at the work of other artists, not to copy them, but so see how they work. Very often, what is left out is just as important as what is put in – space is a very undervalued element in today's music.

Virtually all progress is built on modifying and improving the work of others – very few people are original enough to create something entirely new. Some of the most successful 'new' ideas come from merging existing ideas in unusual ways, and this seems to work particularly well in music. For a number of years now, world music has become integrated into pop music, the unlikely pairing of jazz and rap has inspired new musical directions, and the classics continue to be plundered at all opportunities. In music, the end always justifies the means.

NOTE:

When using sample CDs or CD-ROMs, check the small print for the conditions of use. Most, but not all, commercial sample libraries license the original purchaser to use the samples within a music work without further payment. However, the samples shouldn't be used on their own, and the samples may not be used by third parties. If you have written a potential hit record using samples from someone else's sample library, your best bet is to buy a legitimate copy for yourself to avoid problems.

Never use any copyright material (from other records, TV, radio, live recordings and so on), without written permission from the copyright holder, otherwise you could find your new number one is making money for somebody else and their lawyers, not for you!

chapter 5

effects in the mix

Artificial effects have become an integral part of modern music recording, but it is wrong to think of an effect as something that is added at the last minute to provide a kind of superficial gloss. It is also wrong to assume that using an effect will cover up a mistake or a piece of poor playing, because in most instances, it will simply draw attention to it.

Reverberation needs to be added to most recordings to simulate a natural acoustic environment and as an effect, it occupies a unique position. All other effects are employed for artistic reasons; it helps to plan the type of effect that will be used very early on in a session rather than groping around for something which might or might not work at the last minute. Indeed, some effects form an integral part of the sounds used in a composition, while certain delay-based effects may help determine the rhythm of a piece of music. In the studio, the producer has to decide which effects, if any, need to be added during the recording stage and which can be left until the mix. The home recordist faces the same decisions, though some decisions may be determined by the number of tape tracks and effects units available.

Recording With Effects

Though leaving all effects until the mix gives more room for manoeuvre, it is not always the best way to work, even if the facilities exist to make this practical. Sometimes it helps to record an effect to tape with the original instrument. A good engineer or producer will know instinctively when an effect should be added during recording and when it should be left until the end. Indeed, the very open-endedness of leaving everything to the mix can have a detrimental effect on the production of a piece of music; several producers I've spoken to recently believe it's a good idea to commit yourself to something fairly rigid at an early stage. Failure to do so can lead to a huge amount of time being wasted in exploring different possibilities when all that was needed was a clear sense of direction at the outset. To make matters worse, we now have MIDI sequencers synchronised to tape, mix automation and hard disk digital editing. All these technologies, while wonderful and extremely useful in themselves, can divert much time and effort from the task in hand. Ask anyone who has used an automated mixing system and they'll invariably tell you the mix takes at least twice as long as it did on a manual desk!

Artistic Considerations

When it comes to adding effects, we have to consider both the artistic and logistic effects of either recording them to tape or saving them until the mix. The factors in favour of recording the effect to tape with the original instrument are that:

◆ The player may feel more comfortable and put in a better performance.

◆ Committing effects to tape saves time at the mixing stage...

◆ ... and frees up the effects unit in question for a different task later in the session; for example, a multi-effects unit could provide an echo or delay during recording and then be used to furnish reverb during mixdown.

Conversely, if effects are changed or left out at the recording stage, the original musical performance may no longer work. This is very often the case when delay effects are used, as the musician 'plays' to the effect, but it can apply equally to chorus-type treatments which are often used on guitar parts.

There are negative aspects to recording the effects to tape too, especially if the number of tracks is limited — for example:

◆ Recording an instrument in mono only takes one tape track, but if you want to add an effect, then you need two tape tracks to keep the effect in stereo. You could stick with one track, but that would change the effects level.

◆ Committing effects to tape deprives you of the opportunity to later fine tune the effect, to change its pan position relative to the dry track and to change its level in the mix.

In truth, there are occasions when one or the other approach is most appropriate and it is unwise to develop too rigid a method of working which might deprive you of flexibility when you most need it. If time is limited, recording as many effects as possible while tracking certainly saves time when you come to mix.

Guitar Effects

Guitar parts tend to be recorded with their basic effects, such as overdrive, spring reverb, and expressive pedal effects such as wah wah. Some analogue effects pedals produce a more musical sound than their better specified rackmount counterparts, especially chorus and flange units, while stereo reverb treatments can safely be left to the final mix. Don't be tempted to dismiss an effects pedal purely because of its technical spec — if it sounds good, use it. If it's too noisy, distorts, or causes some other problem, discuss it with the player using the pedal and see if you can simulate the sound with your own equipment. Even if you decide to add the effect at the final mix, you should be able to

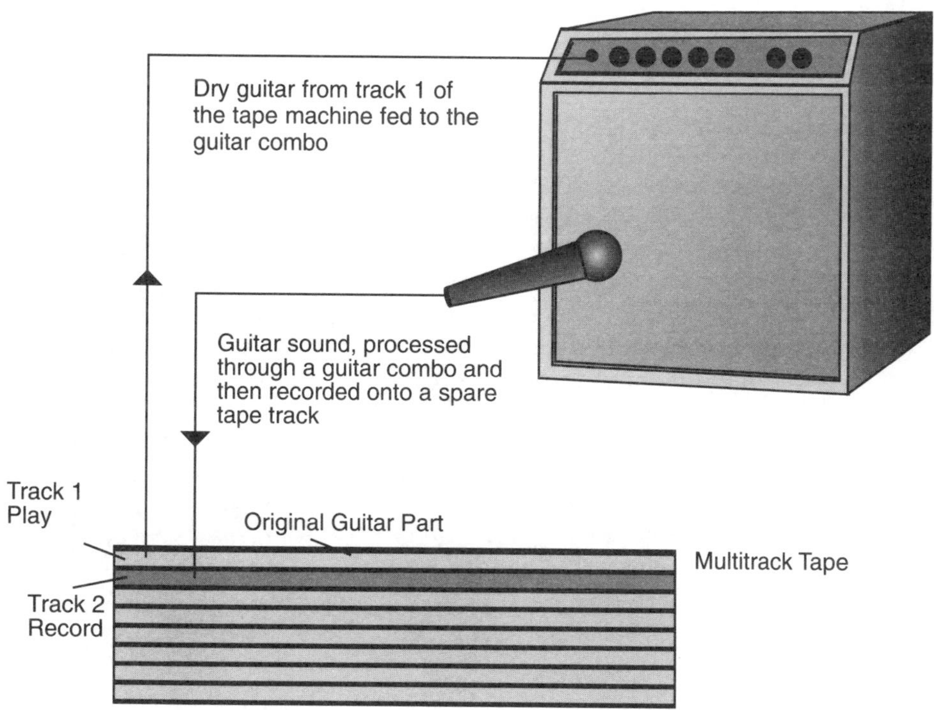

Figure 5.1: Re-recording a Guitar Track via a Combo Amplifier

arrange things so that the player can hear his part with the required effect while playing via the headphone monitoring system. This can usually be achieved by feeding the effect to the monitor mix but without recording it to tape.

★TIP

If it really is necessary to leave a guitar treatment open-ended, it may help to record the sound the player wants on one tape track and a straight, clean, DI'd output from the guitar (via a DI box) on a spare track. This way, it is possible to feed the dry guitar track through an amplifier with the desired effects and overdrive settings, then mic it up, recording the result onto a further spare tape track or over the original guitar part. Figure 5.1 illustrates how this is done.

Logistics

In some circumstances, it is necessary to record effects with the performance purely because there aren't enough effects units or console sends to go around at the mix. Similarly, if tracks have to be bounced together to conserve space on tape, then the necessary effects must be added during the bounce. If track restrictions mean that the bounced signal ends up on a single track, then any added effects will also be mono. This is particularly common in home studios, and the usual outcome is that many of the effects which should have been in stereo end up being in mono. There is no easy way around this, but it is possible to give some semblance of stereo spread to a mono track by processing it at the final mixing stage with an additional stereo reverb treatment. If the track needs little in the way of added reverb, a short, bright plate or an early reflections program will create a sense of depth and width without making the sound seem as though extra reverb has been added at all.

If the main restriction is in the number of console sends, then consider using the channel insert points or direct outputs as sends when adding individual effects to individual tracks. If you have sufficient spare input channels on the mixer, use these as effects returns to enable you to make use of the EQ and pan controls. Ensure that the effects sends are turned down on any channels used as returns or unwanted feedback may result.

Innovative Effects

While most effects can be generated using either dedicated effects units or digital multi-effects processors, it is possible to create something a little out of the ordinary by using just a little ingenuity. Indeed, most of the recordings still regarded as pop classics were made in the days when very few effects units were available and engineers had to improvise. Fine examples can be heard on records by the Beatles and early Pink Floyd to name just two.

Backwards Reverb

Some of the most powerful effects are the most simple to create, and one of my favourites is true 'backwards reverb'. This is quite unlike the canned reverse effects that come as standard on most reverb units, because it actually comes before the sound that caused it. Obviously this can't be done in real life, and it can't be done in real time either, because the reverb unit would have to know what sound was coming next. Nevertheless, it can be done on tape and it is relatively easy.

★TECHNIQUE

◆ Record the original take dry onto the multitrack tape, then turn the tape over so the track plays backwards — from the end of the song to the start. (Turning the tape over also reverses the track order, so that on an 8-track machine, track 1 becomes track 8 and vice versa, so make sure you don't record over any wanted stuff while the tape is reversed.)

◆ With the recording now running backwards, the track to be treated is used to feed a conventional stereo reverb set to a medium to long decay setting (2 to 10 seconds) and the reverb recorded onto an empty track (or pair of tracks if you can afford the luxury of keeping it in stereo).

◆ Once the reverb has been recorded, the tape can be replaced the right way round and played normally. Now the reverb will start to build up a couple of seconds before the track starts and produce an unnatural pre-echo effect. This works very nicely on vocals, but can also be used on instrumental sounds or drums.

◆ Panning the dry sound to one side of the mix and the reverse reverb to the other creates a strong sense of movement, and it is worthwhile experimenting with combined effects such as adding artificial reverse reverb to the track at the same time and panning this to the other extreme.

Ducker

★TECHNIQUE

Another interesting trick is to set up a compressor as a ducker and trigger it from the vocal track. The backwards reverb vocal track is then processed via the ducker so that the reverse effect only surfaces

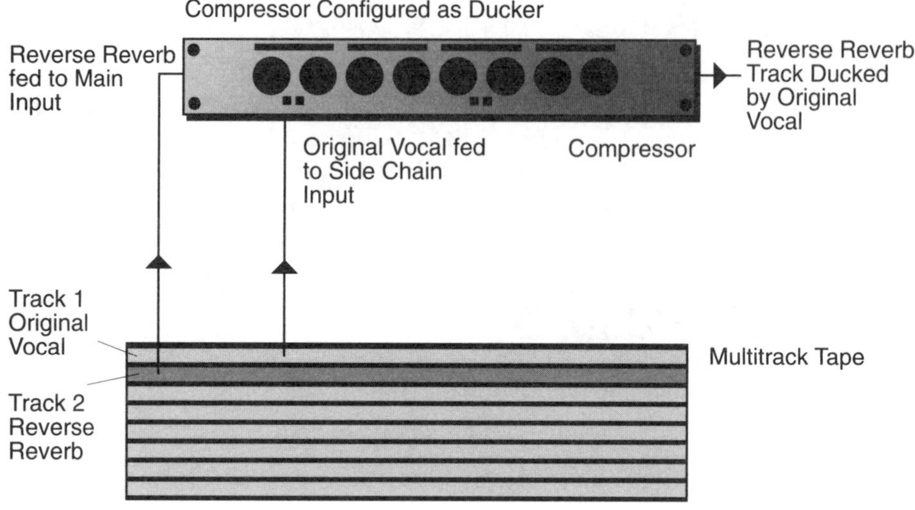

Figure 5.2: Ducked Reverse Reverb

between vocal phrases. This is shown in Figure 5.2. A normal, short reverb can also be added to the vocal track to make it sound natural. The secret is not to overdo it. The reverse sound doesn't have to be used all the way through a song — it can be brought in and out of the mix as required at the touch of a fader.

Pitched Reverb

★TECHNIQUE

Normally, a reverb unit will be fed directly from the track being treated, but there are a couple of tricks that can make the effects more interesting. One technique is to feed the effects send through a pitch shifter before it goes to the reverb unit and drop the pitch by an octave. This means that the original sound will be unchanged but its reverb will be an octave lower than normal. Used on musical sounds, the pitch shift must either be an octave up or an octave down to maintain a true musical relationship, but in the case of drums and percussion, smaller shifts can be used.

Reverb And Flange

★TIP

Flanging is a very dramatic effect but, by the same token, it can be too obvious. However, if we patch in a flanger between the desk's aux send output and the input to the reverb unit, the result is far more subtle than would be achieved by putting the flanger after the reverb output, and helps add sparkle and interest to vocal sounds. This works nicely with synthesized string sounds, as the flanger creates a sense of detail and movement in the reverberant sound without changing the dry part of the sound. And the fact that the flanger comes before the reverb rather than after it means that the cyclic nature of the effect is broken up by the multiple delays of the reverb unit, resulting in a less obvious treatment.

Real Shift

It is well known that pitch shifters can be used to thicken a vocal or instrumental track by providing a slightly detuned version of the original. But, with a little thought, the pitch shifter may be used in a much more convincing way. This technique requires a spare tape track.

★TECHNIQUE

◆ The idea is to double the original vocal part by singing along to the original on tape. Now there's nothing new in this — in fact it's the classic method of double-tracking a line to make it sound fatter or fuller. The difference is that, this time, we take the signal feeding the singer's headphone monitor system and process that through the pitch shifter so that it is between five and ten cents sharp or flat.

◆ The singer now pitches his or her performance to the shifted sound, with the result that the new take is exactly the right amount out of pitch with the first to create a natural chorus effect.

◆ If the pitch shifter has a delay function, a few tens of milliseconds of delay can be added to shift the second take slightly in time as well as pitch. The advantage, apart from having a real as opposed to a synthesized second take, is that the quality of the delay or pitch shifter is totally irrelevant, as the shifted sound isn't used in the recording, only for monitoring.

◆ With instruments, there is no need even to use a pitch shifter — all that is necessary is to change the tape speed slightly, using the varispeed control, and then record a second take without retuning the instrument. Once the tape is replayed at the normal speed, the two slightly out-of-tune takes will produce a chorus effect far more natural than that from any chorus pedal.

chapter 6

vocals

Even those used to working in an all-MIDI environment will need to work with microphones when it comes to getting vocals onto tape. Recording vocals is essentially very simple, but it still surprises me how many people really struggle to get an acceptable vocal sound. In reality, the first necessity is a vocalist who can actually perform well, but taking that for granted, the rest is down to choosing the right type of microphone, putting it in the right position and using the correct degree of compression to control it without choking the life out of it.

Pop shields should be used as a matter of course, and the engineer should have an effective de-essing system available when the singer's vocal characteristics demand one. A suitable reverb or ambience treatment is invariably needed to add realism to vocals recorded in a dead studio, and both the engineer and producer should work to put the singer at his or her ease in order to stimulate the best performance possible.

It is the producer's responsibility to check that the vocal is of sufficient quality throughout and any lines containing errors in either lyrical delivery, timing or pitch should be replaced, ideally during the same session to maintain a continuity of sound. The producer will also need to supervise any harmony parts or double tracking.

Composite Takes

It helps to have photocopies of the lyric sheet on hand before the session gets under way so that the producer can add comments and underline any phrases or words that need patching up as they arise. Some producers are happy to get one reasonable take down on tape and then patch this up by replacing sections, while others prefer to capture several complete takes and then use the best sections from each. In 8- or 16-track studios, the first method is less wasteful of tape tracks and the final mix is easier to handle.

If the singer isn't comfortable singing isolated sections of the song, try running the tape all the way through and simply punching in and out of record on the lines you want to replace. This way, the singer can concentrate on creating a whole performance, even though what you finally use will be the result of several different takes. Even with this method, though, you'll often find that one specific line is giving trouble so you may have to tackle this in isolation until it's right. So long as the singer gets a couple of lines 'run' into it, everyone should be happy.

The second method of producing a composite take — recording several complete takes and then using the best sections from each — is best suited to larger systems; a mixer with mute automation makes it much easier to switch between vocal takes than attempting to do it manually. Often the composite vocal track will be bounced to a spare tape track and the original tracks freed up for re-use. This may mean holding up the session for a while to allow the vocal track to be sorted out but it's one thing less to worry about when you come to mix.

Ultimately, it doesn't matter what method you use, as long as you end up with the vocal take you're happy with. And if that means putting the best vocal chorus into a large-memory sampler and then firing it back into the mix at the appropriate points using MIDI triggering, then that's fine too. After all, this is only the modern equivalent of 'spinning in', where vocal sections such as choruses were transferred to a 2-track open reel machine which was then cued up and started manually to do the same job. This may sound tricky, but if marker pencil cue marks are put on the back of the tape and lined up with some feature on the machine, the results can be quite repeatable.

Vocal Monitoring

Most vocal monitoring is done with headphones, and two types are commonly used. Fully-enclosed headphones are less prone to spillage problems, but some vocalists find that they have trouble singing in tune because the boxed-in feeling distracts them. This is why you often see videos of recording sessions where the singer has one phone on and the other off.

Semi-enclosed phones are more comfortable to work with but they leak more sound, so you could end up with a little of the backing track on the vocal track. This is not normally serious — as long as you don't suddenly decide to use part of the take unaccompanied! The leakage problem may also occur if any sort of click track is being used — basic pulsed tone metronomes tend to spill quite badly.

The quality of monitoring can have a profound effect on the quality of a vocal performance, so take the time needed to set up a good foldback mix for the singer and add sufficient reverb to the headphone mix to make him or her feel comfortable. The room temperature can also affect a singer's ability to pitch — don't automatically blame the singer if something isn't going quite right. A song is only as good as its vocal part, so make every possible effort to keep the singer relaxed and in a creative frame of mind.

The Right Mic

Generally, live vocal mics are dynamic models and incorporate a deliberate treble boost of a few dBs at around 5kHz in order to render the vocal more intelligible. While undoubtedly useful in preserving clarity of diction, such a 'presence peak' is not necessarily a good thing in the studio, where the general aim is to capture as natural a performance as possible.

Most professional studios will use a capacitor mic for vocal use, because these have a high sensitivity and a wide frequency response extending up to 20kHz or so. Dynamic microphones, on the other hand, tend to perform poorly above 16kHz or thereabouts and they are less sensitive than capacitors — which could lead to problems with electronic noise if the vocalist has a quiet voice. However, some rock vocalists prefer to use dynamic mics in the studio because it gives them a fatter sound and they use the mic so close to the mouth that low sensitivity is no longer a problem.

The wide frequency response of capacitor microphones can emphasise sibilance (a whistling sound accompanying S and T sounds) in a performer's voice; the problem is further aggravated by large amounts of compression or bright reverb treatments. The usual cure for sibilance is to use a de-esser to attenuate the sibilant sounds, but in some cases, a more pragmatic approach might be to use a suitable dynamic microphone, as the limited frequency response will tend to hide the problem. It may also be possible to choose a capacitor microphone with a warmer characteristic. This need to match microphone characteristics to vocalists is the main reason a well-equipped studio will have so many different vocal mics.

★TIP

No single microphone is ideal for all vocalists. If a singer has a bright voice, then a mic with a presence peak may tend to make the overall sound appear excessively harsh, whereas the same mic used on a singer with an indistinct or soft voice could yield a significant improvement. Attempting to achieve the same effect by means of EQ seldom succeeds, and for this reason, I would recommend recording vocals with little or no EQ; if the sound isn't right, then try a different mic or change its position slightly before resorting to EQ.

Mic Pattern

Unidirectional or cardioid pattern mics are the preferred choice for live performance because of their ability to reject off-axis sounds, thus minimising both the spill from other performers and acoustic feedback. In the studio, vocals tend to be recorded as separate overdubs where the singer monitors the backing mix via headphones, and in this case the need to use a cardioid pattern mic is not so great. However, unless the studio is acoustically quite dead it may be a good idea to use a directional mic anyway, to minimise the effect of the room acoustics on the recorded sound —

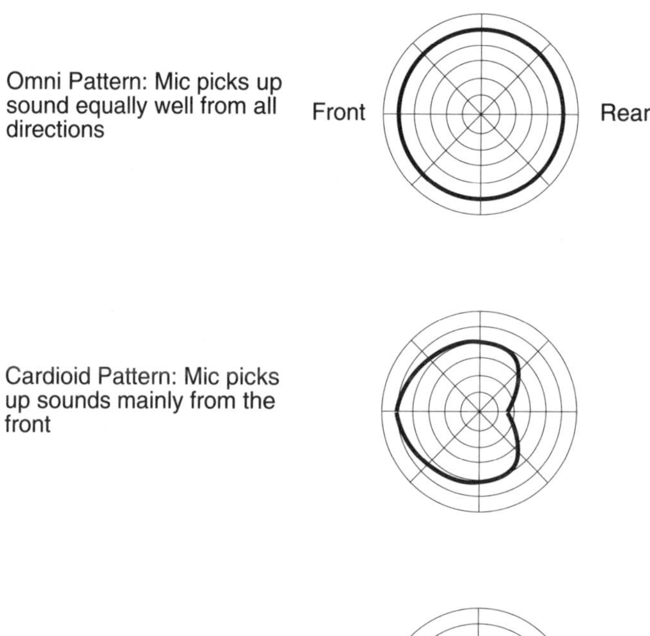

Omni Pattern: Mic picks up sound equally well from all directions
Front
Rear
Cardioid Pattern: Mic picks up sounds mainly from the front
Figure of Eight: Mic picks up sound from front and rear but not from the sides

→TIP

Figure 6.1: The Common Polar Patterns

unless the room acoustics just happen to provide the sound you want. Figure 6.1 shows the directional characteristics available from different types of microphone.

In circumstances where the room does make a positive contribution to the sound (as it may when recording choral music in a church, for example), the result will invariably sound more natural recorded via an omni (omnidirectional) pattern microphone. As a general rule, omni pattern mics produce a more accurate overall picture than an equivalent cardioid because they have the same nominal response in all directions, with the result that both direct and indirect sound is accurately captured.

★TIP

Microphones should be mounted on a solid boom stand and a shock-mount cradle employed if available. However, some singers can't perform properly without a hand-held mic, in which case you should give them one to hold, set up another mic on a stand a couple of feet in front of them, and tell them that you need a mix of the sound from both mics. The recording is invariably made using just the output from the stand-mounted mic!

Pop Shields

Most engineers experience problems with microphone popping, and experience has shown that simple foam wind shields are virtually useless. The popping is caused by blasts of air from the performer's mouth slamming into the microphone diaphragm and giving rise to a high level, low frequency output signal, which comes over as a loud, bassy thump.

Commercial pop filters use a fine plastic or metal gauze stretched over a circular frame somewhere between four and six inches in a diameter and positioned between the performer and the microphone. Normal sound, which consists of vibrations within the air, is not affected, but blasts of moving air are intercepted and their energy dissipated harmlessly as turbulence. Commercial pop shields are very expensive, so here's how to make your own. For the grille, a piece of fine nylon stocking works perfectly. This may be stretched over a wire frame (many engineers use wire coat-hangers) and is then positioned between the microphone and the singer's mouth as shown in Figure 6.2.

A tidier alternative is to use a wooden embroidery hoop to hold the stocking material. Another ready-made option is a frying pan splash guard. These comprise a fine metal mesh fixed to a wire hoop with a handle; the provision of this handle makes it easy to tape the filter to a mic stand.

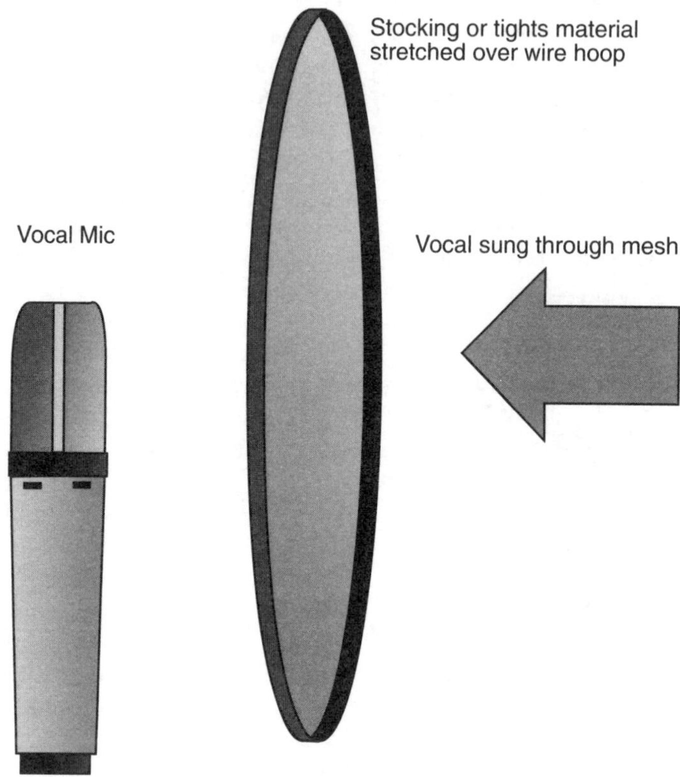

Figure 6.2: Improvised Pop Shield

Mic Positioning

Working too close to a microphone will cause significant changes in both level and tone as the singer moves his or her head. A working distance of between six inches and two feet from the mic is most appropriate to studio work. Most studio vocal recordings are done in a relatively dead environment so that reverb can be added artificially during the mix. In a professional studio, there is likely to be a dedicated vocal booth, but excellent home recordings can be made simply by keeping the microphone well away from the walls of the room and improvising sound absorbers using bedding draped over clothes driers and suchlike. In general, the deader the environment the better, and if the acoustic is still less than ideal, work closer to the mic to improve the ratio of direct to reflected sound.

Vocal Groups

If several vocalists are to be recorded at one time, the distance between mics should be at least three times the distance between the microphone and the vocalist, to avoid phase cancellation effects due to spill. If you can improvise some form of acoustic screening, so much the better.

For larger groups of singers, such as choirs or ensembles, it may be desirable to record them in stereo using a pair of coincident cardioids or an M&S pair. For larger choral recordings, more control is available if you use one stereo pair for each section of the chorus, with the microphone pairs mounted above and in front of the performers.

★TIP

To create the illusion of space when multitracking backing vocals or groups of backing vocalists, try setting up a stereo pair of mics in the room and then moving the performers for each new recording. For example, you could record three tracks with the singers positioned left, then centre, then right of the mics. On playback, this will create the illusion of the three groups of people existing at the same time in a real stereo soundspace. The singers can be made to sound slightly different using established tricks, such as varispeeding the tape slightly for each overdub. These techniques are described later in this chapter when double tracking is explained.

Compression

Compression is invariably needed in pop music production to keep the vocal level nice and even. A degree of compression applied during the recording will help keep the level going onto tape sensibly high and at the same time guard against loud peaks that might otherwise cause tape overload and subsequent distortion. Soft-knee compressors are least obtrusive in this application and should be set to give a gain reduction of 10dB or so during the louder sections. A singer with a very wide dynamic range, on the other hand, may need a ratio type controller set to a ratio of 4:1, or even higher, to really keep the peaks under control. This is where an experienced engineer is a great asset, as he'll know from the first run-through just how much compression will be required. As a rule, choose a fast or programme-dependent attack time and a release time of around half a second.

It is safer to apply less compression than you need, because you can always add more compression when you come to mix. The effect of too much compression added at the recording stage may ruin an otherwise perfect take and will be impossible to correct later. The majority of engineers will use additional compression when mixing, but again you have to take care not to overdo it, because compression also brings out any noise and sibilance present in the recording. The use of an Exciter to brighten a vocal track may also bring up the sibilance to an unacceptable level, in which case you may have to resort to using a de-esser.

A gate or expander is useful to clean up the spaces between words and phrases, but as the setting up is quite critical, these should only be used on the mix and never while recording. That way you can take as many passes as you need to get it right.

Equalisation

Vocals will often need some equalisation to make them 'sit' well with the backing track, while over-sibilant vocals may require dynamic EQ processing using a de-esser. No two singers have exactly the same voice characteristics, so any EQ treatment is likely to be different depending on the singer. However, modifications in certain general areas of the audio spectrum can be considered appropriate to the vast majority of voices, though final EQ settings will have to be tuned by ear with regard to the specific singer being recorded.

◆ Any top boost should be applied quite high up at 6-12kHz, but watch out for sibilance creeping in. However, don't settle for a dull vocal sound simply because using the right EQ brings up the sibilance; if you have to use a de-esser to save the day, then do it.

◆ Boosting in the 1-2kHz range gives a rather honky, cheap sound to the vocals and so is not recommended except as a special effect. I try to keep vocals as flat as possible and tend to use the shelving high control to add just a hint of top rather than anything more drastic.

◆ Presence can be added with just a little boost at 3-4kHz, but be moderate or the sound quality will suffer. After all, vocals are the most natural sound in the world and our ears soon register the fact that they've been tampered with.

◆ If you're mixing several backing vocals, rolling off a touch of bass might help the vocal to sit better in the mix without sounding muddy. On its own, the equalised backing vocal might sound terribly thin, but once in the track, the chances are that it will sound perfectly normal, yet won't fill up the vulnerable lower-mid area of the spectrum with unwanted energy.

Double Tracking

Double tracking is a popular trick used to add depth to a voice. It may be used to compensate for a weak voice, or creatively to add impact to choruses and so on. Traditionally, the singer performs the same part twice (or more) onto two tape tracks and then the two tracks are played back together to give the effect of two singers in unison. Alternative technological tricks may be used to fake the effect, but if a singer is capable of duplicating a performance pretty accurately in pitch and timing, the real way always sounds better.

★TIP

A common problem with double-tracked parts is that words may start together but often sound ragged because the word endings aren't in sync. Nowhere is this more evident than in the case of words ending with 't' or 's' sounds, and a simple dodge is to perform the second take in a deliberately sloppy manner by missing off or fading the ends of tricky words. When the two tracks are played together, the result will sound much tighter. The same applies to backing harmony vocal parts.

★TIP

To create a little difference between the two vocal lines, you could varispeed the multitrack up or down by a semitone or so before recording the second part. This will give the voice a different character when the tape is returned to normal speed; it's a trick often used by radio jingle writers to create the effect of a large vocal group when overdubbing just one or two singers.

★TIP

Another useful trick is to use a delay line to delay the headphone mix by 50mS or so when recording the second track. This has the effect of making the singer perform the second part 50mS later than the first part, giving a short delay effect when the tape is replayed normally. This creates a nice rich effect without compromising the sound quality, because what goes to tape hasn't actually been passed through the delay unit. This means that any old delay will do the trick, even an old tape echo or guitar foot-pedal.

Faking It

Inevitably, some singers can never perform a song the same way twice, in which case any attempt at real double tracking will sound messy and unacceptable. This is where ADT, or Automatic Double Tracking, comes to the rescue. Originally, this effect was created using an open reel machine running at high speed to function as a very short delay unit, or by using the short delay setting on a tape echo unit. By fine-tuning the delay so that the original sound and its repeat just start to separate, you get the effect of two voices singing slightly out of time with each other.

The effect isn't entirely convincing because the pitching of the delayed part is just too perfect, but later electronic attempts to simulate the effect using chorus or pitch shift circuitry can sound rather more realistic:

★TECHNIQUE

◆ A short delay of between 30 and 100mS is added to the sound but the delay is either subtly chorused or processed via a pitch shifter to give a detuning effect of between five and ten cents (one cent is one hundredth of a semitone).

◆ Further depth can be added by panning the original and delayed signals to opposite sides of the stereo mix.

◆ If you only have a basic DDL, then you can use this to simultaneously delay the sound and to vary the pitch — a kind of delayed chorus setting. After getting the delay time right by ear, adjust the modulation depth and speed so that the pitch wavering effect is just audible — a modulation rate of 2-3Hz combined with a very shallow modulation depth should do the trick nicely. The longer the delay time, the less modulation depth you'll need to create the required degree of pitch shifting.

Reverb And Ambience

Even before digital reverb units came along, some way of adding life to vocals had to be found, because the dead studio recording environment made them sound quite lifeless without further treatment. Reverb is part of our everyday lives — we exist in reflective environments, so any sound we hear that is totally devoid of any reverb or ambience sounds unnaturally limp. In the early days, live echo rooms, spring reverb units and echo plates were all used to add reverberation to recordings, the most successful probably being the plate. This comprised a large steel plate suspended in a rigid frame and driven into vibration by a voice coil similar to that on a loudspeaker. The resulting vibrations were picked up by two or more surface-mounted contact mics and amplified before being fed back into the mix. The final effect was brighter than natural reverb, but it was a musically pleasant sound, which is why most modern digital units have plate simulation modes as well as rooms, halls and chambers. Figure 6.3 shows how a plate works.

Picking the right reverb setting is where the producer's artistic input is vital, because there are many ways of approaching any musical project,

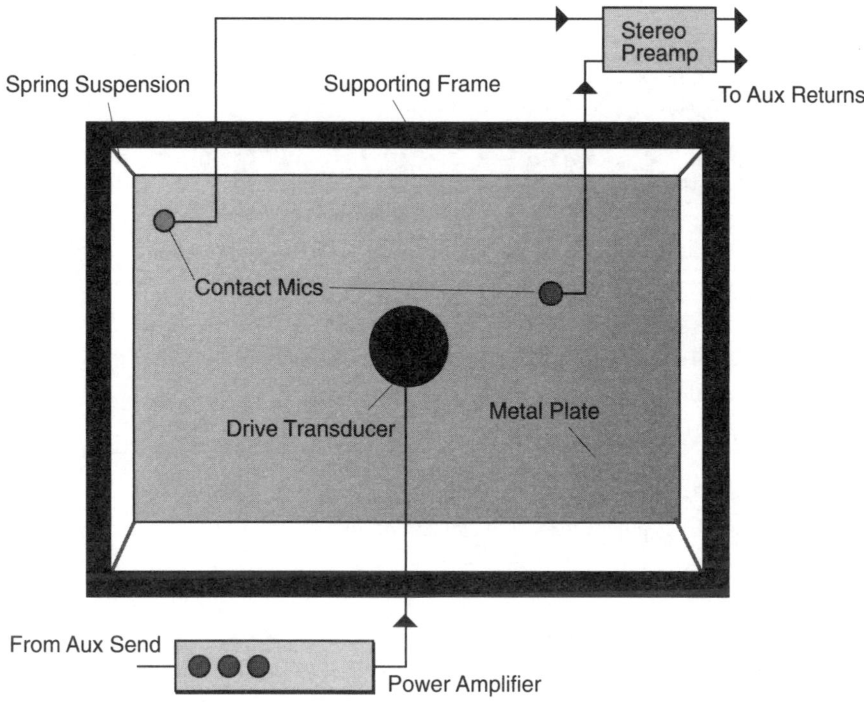

Figure 6.3: Reverb Plate

with no particular way being more right than others. Even so, there are a few guidelines based largely on common sense:

◆ Bright reverb settings give the vocal an attractive 'sizzle', as long as they are not so bright as to bring the level of sibilance up to an unacceptable degree.

◆ If the song is a ballad, a longer, softer reverb might create a more appropriate atmosphere.

◆ Short ambience settings, rich in early reflections, can be used to add life to a vocal while adding no perceptible reverb at all, and trick settings such as reverse reverb also have their place if used in moderation.

Advanced Effects

You can create a useful effect by setting a DDL to give a single repeat

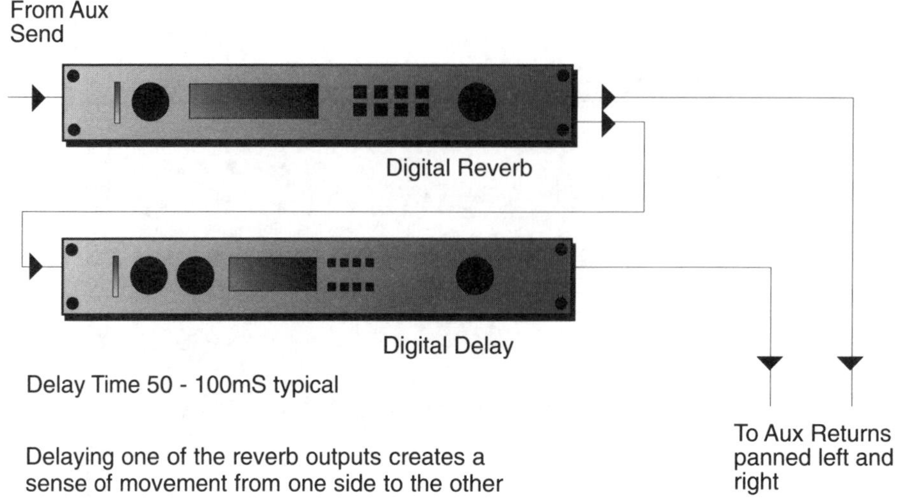

Figure 6.4: Delaying One Reverb Output

between 50 and 100mS long, and feed this into a reverb unit to give a pre-delay. This creates a deeper sense of space and also separates the reverb from the basic sound a little, which can enhance the clarity. Many multi-effects units have a pre-delay setting included in the reverb parameters, but this little dodge is still useful for those occasions where your main reverb unit is tied up on another job and you have to create an effect using something pretty basic.

★TIP

Another production trick can be achieved by putting a delay after the reverb but on only one of the stereo outputs. This splits the reverb so that it starts in one speaker and then moves over to the other. Once again, this treatment adds a sense of movement but without becoming too obvious or gimmicky. Figure 6.4 shows how this might be arranged.

Reverb Panning

Reverb panning can also be used to create movement and interest without actually giving the game away, and if your multi-effects unit includes a panner, panning the output of the reverb unit from left to right, ideally at a rate that fits in with the tempo of the song, can be very effective. If you don't have a panner, you can create the same effect by using a gate such as the Drawmer DS201 which has side-chain or key inputs.

★TECHNIQUE

◆ Using two sounds programmed into a drum machine (this must have at least two assignable outputs), the two sides of the gate can be triggered alternately via the key inputs. Ideally, the drum machine would be synchronised to the master tape using a MIDI sequencer.

◆ The stereo reverb is then fed into the main gate inputs and the attack and release times set to give a smooth pan effect. This only takes a little trial and error and is remarkably effective.

◆ If you have two reverb units, try a reverse setting on one of the reverb units and a conventional reverb setting on the other. Pan one reverb unit left and the other right and you'll find that as the normal reverb decays on one side, the reverse effect will build up on the other, giving a different kind of moving pan effect.

A Matter Of Taste

Almost any effect, no matter how bizarre, can be justified in context — it's all a matter of artistic judgment, which is where a good producer comes into his or her own. I've even heard vocals chopped into short, gated sections and then panned between the speakers, giving an effect like a synchronised, intermittent mic cable fault, but because it was used sparingly and in the right place, it worked. Similarly, a good vocal line can be completely ruined by the gratuitous application of effects. In most cases, clarity of diction is important, in which case the longer the reverb decay time, the lower its level should be in the mix or the sound will become muddled.

Art Before Technology

By all means combine two or more different reverb units to create a composite effect that enhances the vocal sound, but always keep your artistic aims at the front of your mind and don't let the technology dictate your actions. The technology is there to serve you, not the other way around. Most pop songs rely on a strong, distinctive vocal part and it is up to the producer to achieve that by whatever means possible.

Finally, artists tend to ask for effects they have heard before and many are over-used cliches such as adding repeat echo to the last word in a vocal line or the last word in a song. Occasionally, one of these cliches may still be OK to use, but it is far better to do the unexpected than kill your record with predictability. If you must use a cliche, try to use it in an unexpected way or in an unusual place. For example, adding a gross repeat echo to the very first word in a song might have more impact than using it right at the end.

chapter 7

drums

It's probably true to say that now, more than ever, pop records are being made using electronically sequenced drum sounds rather than the real thing. Fashions have a habit of changing, however, and a good engineer should be prepared for all eventualities. The ability to record a real drum kit is a vital skill that no engineer should be without, for even if the majority of work is done with electronic percussion, it is still common practice to overdub real cymbals and percussion to add a spark of humanity to the end result.

The Kit

Provided the kit to be recorded is well looked after and fitted with decent heads, it should be possible to get a good sound out of it within half an hour or so. Old heads stretch unevenly and the surface becomes wrinkled, causing a loss of tone which no amount of tuning and damping will fix. Contrary to popular belief, drum tuning doesn't have to be radically changed for recording; a little careful damping is often all that is needed. Furthermore, most drum recording is done using relatively inexpensive dynamic mics, making it possible to mic the entire kit for around the same price as a couple of good vocal mics.

The easiest kit to record is the one that uses single-headed toms. If the toms are double-headed, the bottom heads may normally be removed without problems, though you may find that the nut boxes rattle; a little inventive work with a pack of Blu Tak will usually cure this. If you prefer the sound of the toms double-headed, they do require more critical tuning, and the bottom head often needs a little careful damping to prevent it ringing.

Tuning And Damping

Snare drums usually have metal or wooden shells, though some make use of synthetic materials, and they vary in depth enormously. Metal shells give a brighter tone with quite a lot of ring, while wooden snares tend to be warmer. Whatever the type, it is important to ensure that the snares are in good order and properly adjusted to minimise rattling.

Usually the snare head is tensioned slightly looser than the batter head, though individual drummers will have their own ideas on tuning. As a starting point, all drum heads should be tensioned as evenly as possible; tapping the head around the edges should give the same pitch all the way around the head. Every drum has a natural range of tuning and it will be evident if the tuning is too far out, as the tone will be either too hard or very lifeless.

Inevitably, the snares will vibrate in sympathy whenever another drum is hit, and though this may be minimised by careful tuning of the snare drum relative to the rest of the kit, it can seldom be eliminated completely. One approach is to gate the snare mic, but this does nothing to remove the buzz picked up by the overhead mics. Some engineers resort to taping coins onto the snare head to pull the head down onto the snares, but in my experience, this compromises the tone of the drum.

An undamped drum has a surprisingly long decay time and, what's worse, it will ring in sympathy whenever other drums are hit. Overdamping, on the other hand, can leave a kit sounding lifeless, yet many inexperienced engineers choke the life out of a kit because they are worried by minor rings and rattles that would probably be inaudible in the context of a complete mix anyway. A little experience will soon show the right amount of damping to use. Internal dampers are rarely used in the studio as they put pressure on the head. Far better to use a pad of tissue or cloth held in place with a strip of studio tape.

One trick often used to give a more dynamic tom sound is to first tune the head evenly, but then slacken off just one tuning lug a touch. This produces a slight pitch drop after the drum is struck, rather like an electronic drum, with the effect related to how hard the drum is hit.

★TIP

Most contemporary drummers will have a hole cut in the front head of the kick drum which makes miking very easy, though the hole should be as large as is practical to prevent the remaining material from ringing excessively. Don't be tempted to remove the front head completely, as this can put uneven stress on the drum shell and may cause it to distort. A wooden bass drum beater gives a better-defined sound than cork or felt beaters, and a patch of mole skin or hard plastic taped to the head where the beater hits will add more of a click to the sound. There are specialist drum products for this application, but an old credit card works perfectly well.

★TIP

Damping the bass drum is best achieved by placing a folded woollen blanket inside the drum so that it rests on the bottom of the shell and touches the lower part of the rear head. Further damping is unlikely to be necessary, though noise gates are often used to sharpen up the decay of the sound.

Miking Options

Perhaps the most accurate way to mic a drum kit is with a stereo microphone pair (either coincident or spaced) placed between five and ten feet in front of the kit. This arrangement can capture the live sound of the kit very faithfully, but the degree of artistic success is dependent on the actual sound and balance of the drum kit and on the suitability of the room acoustics. If the snare and kick drum need to be made more assertive, additional close mics can be used on these and added to the mix, usually

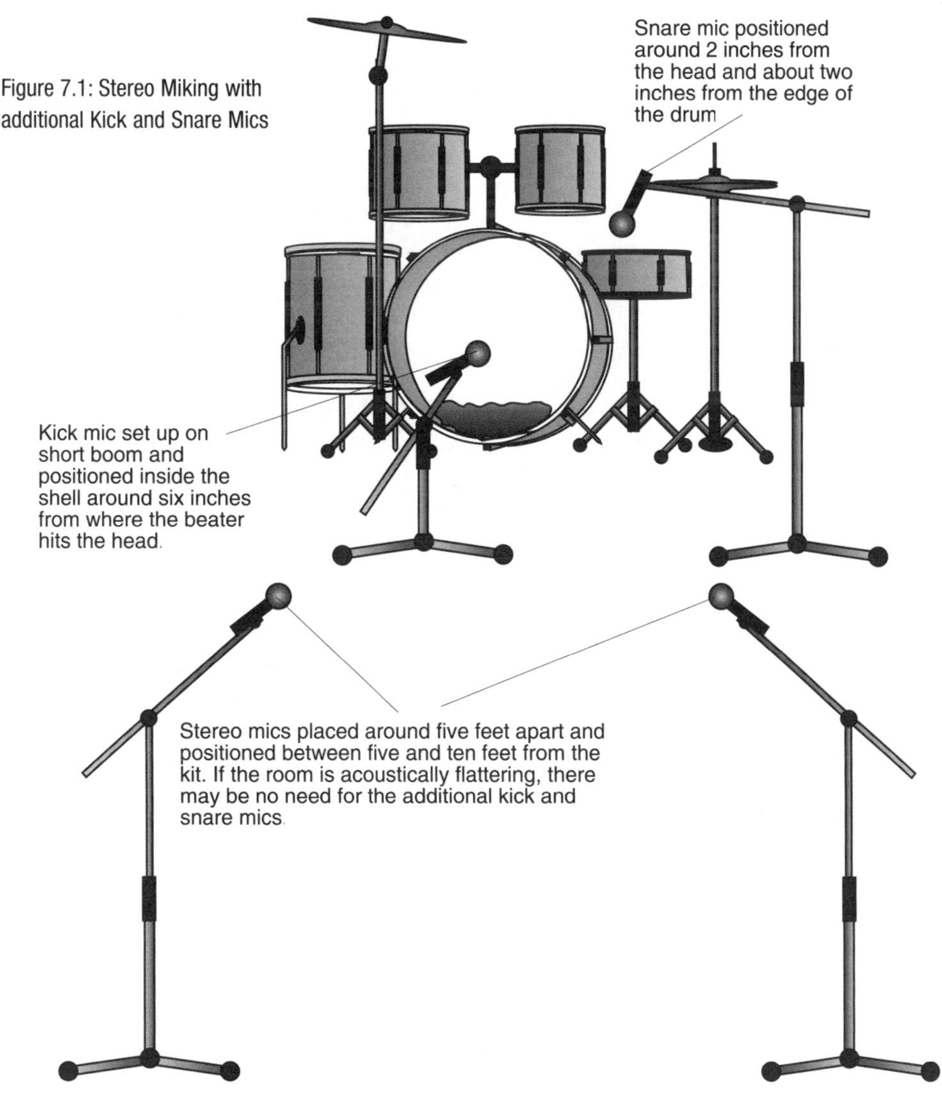

Snare mic positioned around 2 inches from the head and about two inches from the edge of the drum
Kick mic set up on short boom and positioned inside the shell around six inches from where the beater hits the head.
Stereo mics placed around five feet apart and positioned between five and ten feet from the kit. If the room is acoustically flattering, there may be no need for the additional kick and snare mics.

Figure 7.1: Stereo Miking with additional Kick and Snare Mics

panned to the centre. The mic positions will be similar to those used when a separate mic is used on each drum. This set-up is illustrated in Figure 7.1.

This method of miking is not suitable for situations in which spill from other instruments might cause a problem. Furthermore, for pop music work, the natural sound of the kit is often the last thing the producer wants to hear, though it has applications in jazz and suchlike! More often, the kit is recorded with closely positioned mics on the individual drums, with an additional stereo pair located above the kit to capture the ambience.

Close Miking

◆ SNARE AND TOMS:

Snare drums produce the brightest sound in the kit other than the cymbals, so a dynamic mic with a respectable top end or a capacitor mic is desirable. Most engineers use cardioid pattern mics for all the drums, to give the greatest immunity from spill, but in reality, omni mics don't fare much worse than cardioid in this respect and have the benefit of picking up off-axis sounds more accurately. In other words, they may pick up a touch more spill from the other drums, but at least they'll pick it up accurately. A further benefit is that omni mics don't suffer from the proximity effect and so are less susceptible to unpredictable tonal changes when used close to an instrument, as is the case when miking drums. The usual mic position for the snare and toms is a couple of inches above the drum head, a couple of inches in from the edge and angled towards the centre of the head. Any damping should be positioned so as not to be between the mic and the drum.

◆ KICK DRUM:

Kick drum mics are invariably mounted on boom stands so that the mic can be positioned inside the drum shell. A good starting position is with the mic pointing directly at the point on the head where the beater hits it and at a distance of six inches or so. By changing the distance slightly or moving the mic to one side, a significant tonal change can be achieved, giving the engineer a means of controlling the sound at source rather than using EQ. Because of the low frequencies involved, a mic with a good bass response is essential, and it must be able to stand the high sound levels that occur inside a kick drum. Dynamic cardioids or figure-of-eights tend to be used in this role.

◆ CYMBALS:

Capacitor mics should be used as overhead/ambience mics to preserve the transient detail of the cymbals; depending on the kit set-up, you may find a separate hi-hat mic useful, especially if the close drum mics are to be gated. For the hi-hat mic, a position a few inches from the edge of the

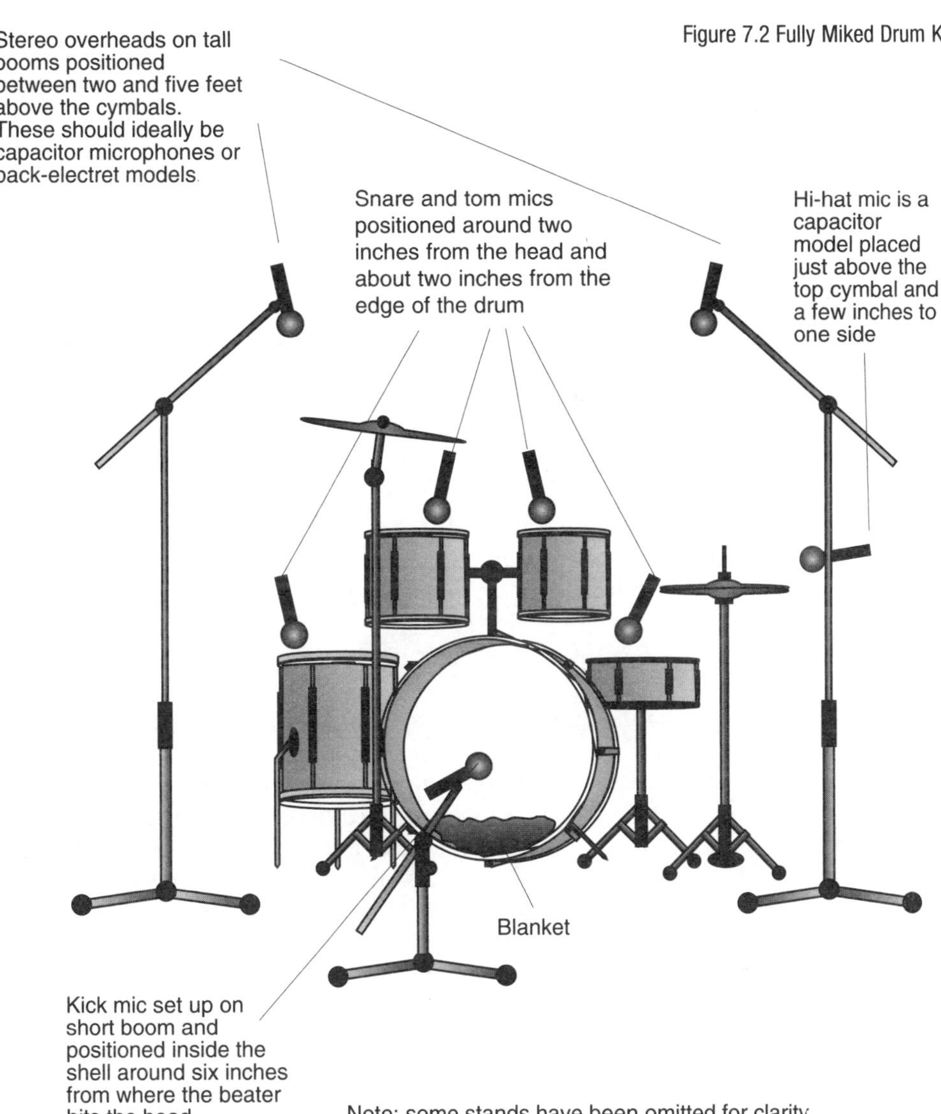
Stereo overheads on tall booms positioned between two and five feet above the cymbals. These should ideally be capacitor microphones or back-electret models.
Snare and tom mics positioned around two inches from the head and about two inches from the edge of the drum
Hi-hat mic is a capacitor model placed just above the top cymbal and a few inches to one side
Blanket
Kick mic set up on short boom and positioned inside the shell around six inches from where the beater hits the head.
Note: some stands have been omitted for clarity
Figure 7.2 Fully Miked Drum Kit

cymbals and angled from above or beneath will avoid the mic picking up the sound of air being expelled when the cymbals are closed. Figure 7.2 shows a fully miked kit.

◆ PERCUSSION:

General percussion such as congas may be miked from overhead in either mono or stereo, and unless separation is a problem, the mic distance may be increased to anywhere between one and three feet from the drum.

In situations where the mics are placed at a distance, the room will have more of an influence on the sound, whereas close miking will capture little of the room ambience, giving a drier sound which may be processed further during mixing.

Tracking

The number of tape tracks allocated to the drum kit depends on the total number of tracks at your disposal and on the requirements of the rest of the instrumentation. Ideally, six tracks should be considered a minimum, divided up as kick, snare, stereo toms and stereo overheads. Check that the overheads are panned the same way as the tom mics! If spare tracks are abundant, then a separate track for each tom might be useful, though in the smaller studio, there may be only four tracks, or even fewer, reserved for drums. In this case, it may be advantageous to mix the bass drum and snare drum together on one track and all the toms on another, keeping just the overheads in stereo. Providing a significant amount of the stereo overhead signal is used in the mix, some degree of stereo imaging will be restored.

Machines And Samples

Drum machines provide an easy way of obtaining high quality drum sounds, though they need to be programmed by someone with a good feel for percussion if the end result is to be acceptable. Many sequencer users prefer to use their drum machines or samplers merely to provide the sounds, the actual programming being done by playing the drum part in real time either from a MIDI keyboard or some form of MIDI drum pad system. Usually, the part is built up in layers rather than all in one go, and it helps to hold the timing together if a straight guide rhythm is recorded first. This may be quantised, if necessary, before the rest of the drum part is added and then deleted once the recording is complete.

Even the best drum machines sound less than convincing when playing fast tom fills because each beat produces exactly the same sound, unlike a real kit which has subtle variations in tone. For this reason, some producers prefer to program the kick drum and snare parts but play the hi-hats, cymbals and toms on acoustic drums miked conventionally. This eliminates problems such as sympathetic resonances in the bass drum or snare rattles and improves separation, allowing a cleaner result to be obtained. The slight timing errors of a real player make the whole thing sound more human, but the overall sound is cleaner and the essential rhythm elements, the kick and snare, can be made as tight as is desired.

Drum Sound Replacement

Drum samples can also be used to replace sounds on tape which have been properly played but where the sound is inadequate in some way. This technique relies on the drums being recorded on separate tracks, but on most sessions, at least the kick and snare drums will have their own track.

★TECHNIQUE

◆ If tape tracks are limited, gate the sounds while recording to isolate them from any spill; for this application, gates with key filters cope much better than straightforward gates. If there are plenty of available tape tracks, record the drums onto individual tracks and then gate afterwards. This allows more than one take if the gate settings are not properly optimised.

◆ The output from the gate should then be fed into a pad-to-MIDI converter, though some drum modules have these built in. However, it is

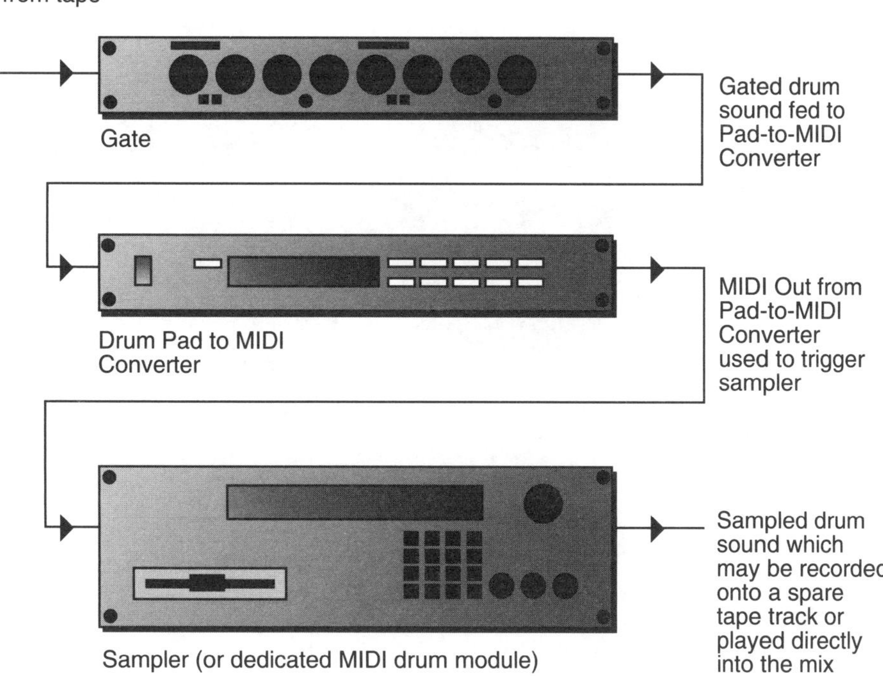

Figure 7.3: Replacing Drum Sounds with Samples

essential that the trigger system allows the user to set a retrigger inhibit time, which prevents a sample from being triggered twice in quick succession due to spill breakthrough or a careless stick bounce. Most trigger systems can be made responsive to the loudness of the triggering signal, but in the majority of pop work, the bass and snare levels need to be kept even, so it may be advantageous to turn this facility off or make sure that the input is always high enough to ensure the sample is played at or near its maximum velocity. Figure 7.3 shows a typical set-up.

Figure 7.4: DIY Piezo Drum Transducer

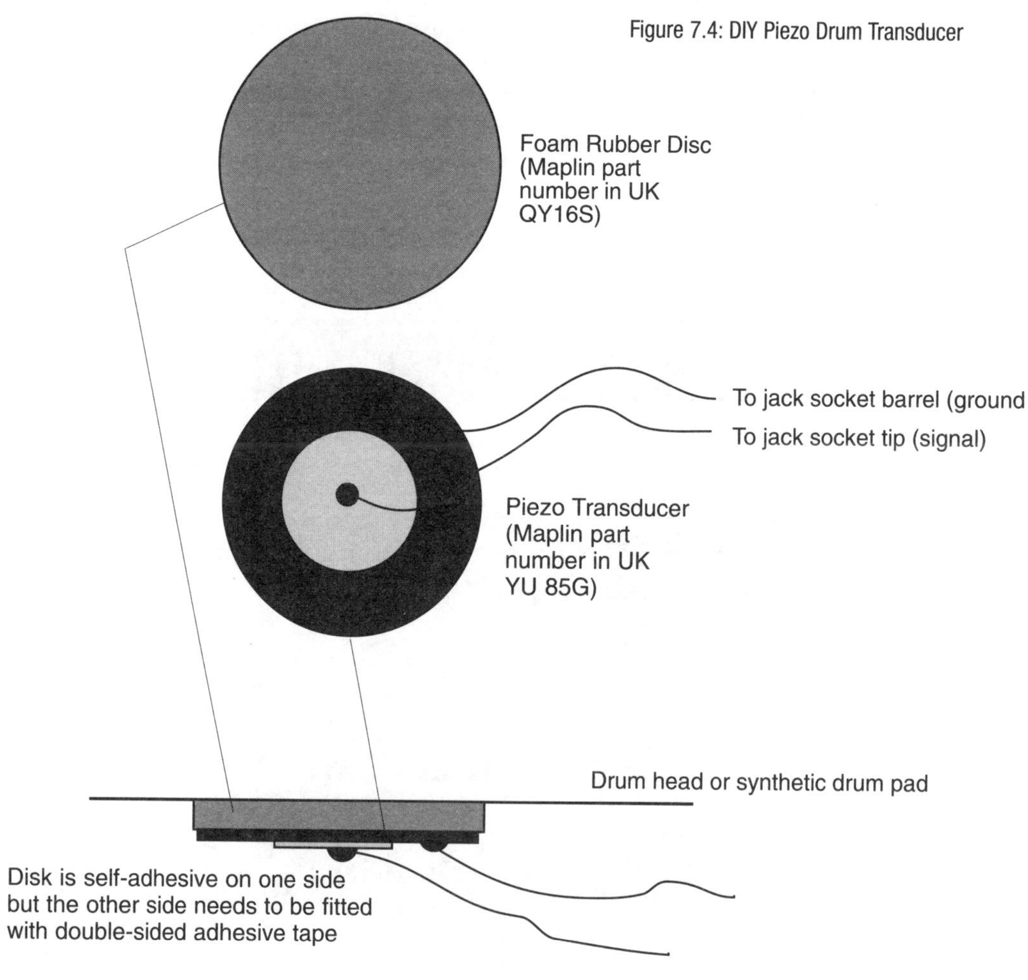

Pads

Drum pads provide a convenient means of triggering sampled drum sounds or sounds generated from a drum machine or drum sound module which, especially in the home studio, are less problematic to record than real drums. Pads, played with sticks, invariably allow a more natural feel to be imparted to the playing than is obtained by playing drum parts from a keyboard, and they allow drummers to become involved in sequencer programming rather than leaving it all to the keyboard player. Inexpensive transducers are also available which may be attached to acoustic drums, allowing them to be used in place of pads. Most types are based around simple piezo-electric transducer disks or it is possible to make your own using piezo-electric sounders (normally used as computer bleepers) attached to the drum head by means of a double-sided foam sticky pad. These may be obtained from a variety of electrical component suppliers at very low cost. Figure 7.4 shows how this is done.

While it is commonplace to quantise bass drum and most snare drum parts, it helps to maintain a natural feel if drum fills are left unquantised. When working with a sequencer, it is usually easiest to program drum parts in layers rather than trying to record the whole kit at once, unless you have a set of pads that includes a kick drum and hi-hat pedal. Each pass can be recorded on a different track and then merged when all the parts are complete. As ever, it helps to get the straight rhythmic parts, such as the kick and snare, down first and then overdub the hi-hats, cymbals and fills. If this isn't practical, program a simple guide rhythm and then erase this later.

In order to preserve the feel of the unquantised parts, the quantised parts should be recorded onto one sequencer track and the unquantised parts onto another — if you put them all on the same track, the same quantisation will apply to everything, which is not what you want. My earlier comments regarding mixing programmed and miked drum sounds apply equally when using pads. Natural hi-hats can often help tremendously when trying to make a programmed part sound convincing

Drum pads are also ideal for playing tuned percussion such as vibes and marimbas, where only a small selection of notes is required.

★TIP

When triggering drum samples, it is also possible to create convincing talking drum effects by creating a looped sequencer track containing only pitch bend information on the same MIDI channel as the drum samples.

When the drum part is played from either the pads or the sequencer, the bend information is merged with the note data and produces the talking drum effect. Creating the bend information requires a little trial and error but is best done with a typical drum part playing so that the effect can be heard. Subtle pitch bends work best, and if the loop is made an odd length, the pitch bend pattern will appear to be constantly changing. I have used this technique very successfully to make sampled congas sound more like tablas.

chapter 8

acoustic guitars

Steel-strung acoustic guitars are wonderfully expressive instruments, and their sound encompasses almost all the audio spectrum, with the exception of the lowest couple of octaves. The instrument also has a very wide dynamic range, and while an enthusiastically strummed rhythm part might be relatively loud, a melodic section played with the fingers or with a pick might sound very much quieter. Because of the wide range of acoustic guitars, both in terms of frequency and dynamics, you should use the very best mic you can get your hands on when recording a critical acoustic guitar part. Some of the better dynamic microphones are sensitive enough for all but the quietest playing, but the higher sensitivity of a capacitor model is a distinct advantage. Similarly, the extended frequency range of a capacitor microphone is better able to capture the subtle high frequency detail of the instrument.

Not everyone can afford a top quality capacitor microphone, but a modestly priced back-electret microphone can do almost as good a job for around the same price as a decent dynamic microphone. Further down the scale, even the humble Tandy PZM is capable of creditable results in this application, its main limitation being its lack of sensitivity when compared to a professional studio capacitor microphone.

Mic Positions

If getting enough level while recording an acoustic guitar is proving a problem, it is tempting to put the microphone very close to the sound-hole. This produces the largest signal, but unfortunately, the tone is likely to be heavily coloured by body resonances, and tends to be both dull and boomy. These body resonances are part of the natural timbre of the instrument and are what gives the guitar sound its depth, but the essential detail that completes the picture comes from elsewhere. No amount of equalisation can make a good guitar sound out of a bad one, and the key to a good sound is to use the right mic in the right position.

As with all instruments, the various parts of the guitar vibrate in different ways; different parts of the instrument generate different sounds. The strings, the neck vibration, the air within the body and the wood of the body itself all contribute to the overall sound. Add to this the effect of room acoustics and it's easy to see why a single microphone positioned close to one point on the instrument's surface is not going to do it justice; this is why contact mics rarely give a good sound.

It could be argued that the only place you're going to get a good guitar sound is where the audience would normally be — several feet from the guitar. Fortunately, you can get good results far closer than this — after all, the guitarist himself usually hears a passable sound and he's quite close. On top of that, the sound we want to record isn't necessarily the exact sound the audience would hear at a live performance.

Tone

A steel-strung acoustic rhythm guitar may need to be both brightened and have some bass rolled off to make it sit better in the mix without taking up too much 'space'. Conversely, a solo acoustic guitar is normally miked to sound fairly natural, but even then, the performer may want to vary the sound slightly, either by the choice and positioning of microphones, by the use of equalisation or by some form of electronic enhancement.

The Right Microphone

Foremost when recording an acoustic guitar is the choice of microphone, because if the chosen model is insufficiently sensitive or has a restricted frequency response, this reduces our options when we come to position it. Most dynamic microphones are not sufficiently sensitive to do justice to the acoustic guitar, and their lack of top end response leads to a somewhat lifeless sound. However, if a dynamic mic is all you have, you can still get passable results by taking a little extra care. Don't point it directly at the sound-hole in an attempt to get enough level, and by the same token, don't place it too close to the guitar. A position between 12 and 18 inches from the guitar is quite near enough and if you're only using a single dynamic mic, then try aiming it at the point where the neck joins the body. You may end up with a little noise but better that than a dreadful sound. Figure 8.1 shows this approach.

Ideally, a capacitor or back-electret mic should be used for any serious work and either omni or cardioid pattern models may be used. Unless the room acoustics are particularly flattering, I'd be inclined to stick to a cardioid model — unless two guitars are being recorded together, in which case it may be better to use omnis rather than cardioids. This will result in a little more spill between the mics, but because omnis tend to have a better off-axis response than cardioids, the spill will at least be sonically accurate.

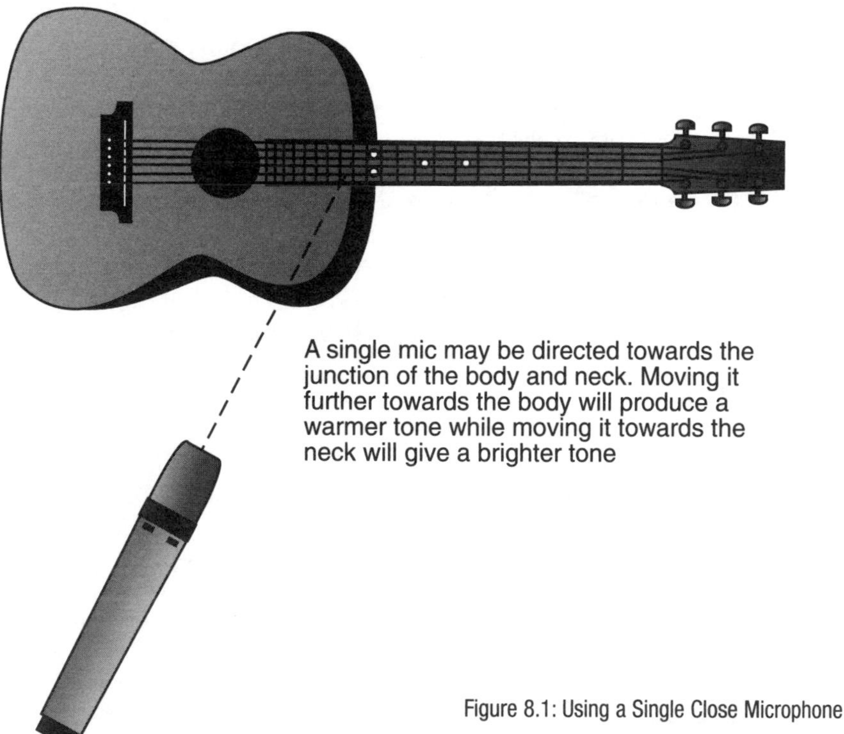

A single mic may be directed towards the junction of the body and neck. Moving it further towards the body will produce a warmer tone while moving it towards the neck will give a brighter tone

Figure 8.1: Using a Single Close Microphone

When using multiple microphones, try to keep in mind the 'three to one' rule for mic positioning. For example, if the mics are placed two feet from the guitars, then make sure they are at least six feet apart. If they are too close to each other relative to their distance from the instruments, the resulting spill will produce significant phase cancelling effects that will colour the sound, usually to its detriment. Getting the desired tone by choosing a suitable mic and mic position always sounds better than using EQ, and if you need a brighter tone, choosing a mic with a presence peak will invariably give a more natural result than applying EQ.

Before The Session

Unlike electronic keyboards, you can't just assume that a guitar is going to play properly and in tune as soon as it comes out of the box. Intonation problems and buzzes should be fixed before the session starts, and with steel-strung instruments, a relatively new set of strings is a good idea, particularly if you're after a bright sound.

The performer should, ideally, play seated to avoid unnecessary movement of the guitar relative to the microphones. Ensure that the chair doesn't creak and try to exclude other sources of noise such as spill from headphones, especially if you intend to work with a click track. A degree of finger squeak is inevitable, but if it becomes excessive, it can ruin an otherwise excellent performance. There's no complete cure but a dusting of talcum powder on the player's hands might improve matters. There are also commercial string lubricants that may help. Other unwelcome sources of noise include rustling clothing, crackling lyric sheets and excessive breathing noises. Also keep an ear open for ticking watches. It can be argued that breath noises are normal, but if you have several overdubs to do, the result can sound like a chorus of heavy-breathing, dirty phone callers!

Click Tracks

When working with click tracks, choose a sound for your click that isn't too strident, as some spill is likely, even from enclosed phones. You could route the click signal through a compressor set up in 'duck' mode so that the click track gets louder when the guitar is played louder and quietens down during quiet sections or pauses. This will ensure that the click is audible to the performer at all times, but it will be quietest when there is little else going on to hide it.

★TIP

There are also some processing tricks which help minimise recorded squeaks and breathing, which will be discussed later in this chapter.

Rooms And Mic Positions

Before getting down to the finer points of microphone placement, it is helpful to look at the surroundings in which the recording is to be made. Most instruments are designed to sound best when played in a room with a certain degree of reverberation, and acoustic guitars are no exception. However, most small studios tend to be on the acoustically dead side, so it may pay dividends to look for another room in the building that has hard surfaces to create a more live environment. In the absence of a suitable live room, an artificial live environment can be created by covering the floor with hardboard, shiny side up.

★TIP

Don't worry if the sound still isn't as live as you'd like it to be, as some electronic reverberation can be added at the mixing stage.

As stated earlier, I really can't overemphasise the importance of microphone position when recording acoustic instruments. That's not to say that there's only one right way to do the job, though — there are many different miking methods that produce excellent results. As shown in Figure 8.1, placing a single mic between one and two feet from the instrument, pointing toward the spot where the neck joins the body, is always a good starting point. If the sound is too heavy, the mic can be positioned further away from the sound-hole or moved upwards so that it is 'looking down' on the instrument. To add more weight to the sound, the mic can be brought closer to the sound-hole, but make sure that the sound doesn't become boomy as well as full.

This is by no means the only mic position — I've had quite a lot of success pointing the mic over the player's right shoulder, looking down on the guitar body from a distance of between 18 inches and two feet. The theory here is that if the guitar sounds OK to the player, it should sound OK to a mic located close to the player's ear. Figure 8.2 shows this set-up. Equally, you might find that pointing the mic at the floor to pick up mainly reflected sound gives a well balanced result.

A good engineer will move around the playing position as the performer warms up, listening for any 'sweet spots'. This careful

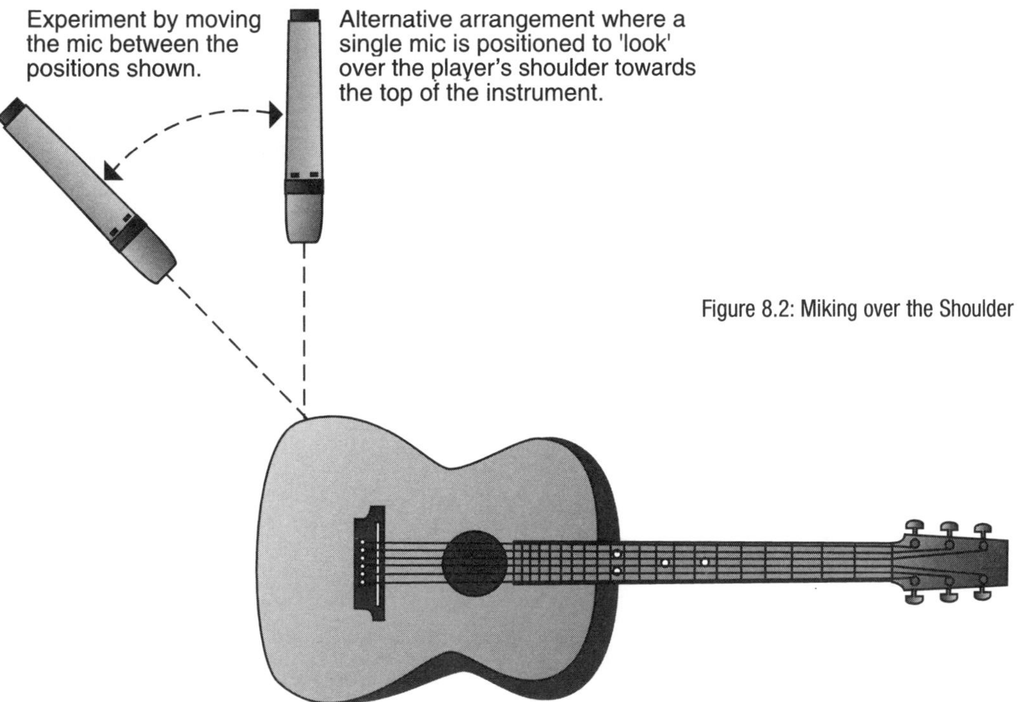

Experiment by moving the mic between the positions shown.
Alternative arrangement where a single mic is positioned to 'look' over the player's shoulder towards the top of the instrument.

Figure 8.2: Miking over the Shoulder

listening invariably yields some improvement, and when you've identified these 'sweet spots', try moving the mic to hear what difference it makes.

★TIP

One effective way to find sweet spots is to monitor the output from the mic using good quality closed headphones plugged into the mixer. You then move the mic manually as the guitarist runs through the number. This has the advantage that any coloration of the sound by the microphone or mixing console is taken into account.

Mono Or Stereo?

If an acoustic guitar line is simply part of a full pop mix, then a mono recording is generally adequate and may even be beneficial as it produces a more stable, solid sound. However, in small acoustic bands or in the case of solo performances, stereo miking greatly enhances the sense of depth and reality. The easiest way to make a stereo recording is to place a stereo pair of microphones two or three feet in front of the instrument, but in practice, you can use any of the existing stereo miking methods, including M&S pairs, spaced microphones or spaced PZMs.

I'll often pick two mic positions that don't necessarily produce an accurate stereo picture as such, but do provide me with the sound I want, plus a sense of depth. One arrangement that I find works particularly well is to position one mic in the usual end-of-neck or 'looking down' position to capture the main part of the sound and then position another a foot or so away from the neck, pointing towards the headstock or halfway up the neck. This produces a bright, detailed sound that works particularly well with picked or folk-style playing. I'd normally use cardioid mics, but you could use omnis if they are available, or even one of each. It really doesn't matter how you get a result so long as you get it! Figure 8.3 shows how the microphones are arranged.

Using two PZM mics, you can obtain a very natural sound by placing these on a table top a couple of feet in front of the performer, with the mics three feet or so apart. Alternatively, these could be set up as a conventional stereo pair, as outlined in the chapter on stereo mic techniques. Even inexpensive Tandy PZMs can sound surprisingly good when placed on a low table in front of the performer. Alternatively, if a guitar is fitted with a bridge transducer, this may be used in conjunction with either one or more microphones to create a stereo effect, though I've never really liked the sound of transducers when compared directly to good microphones.

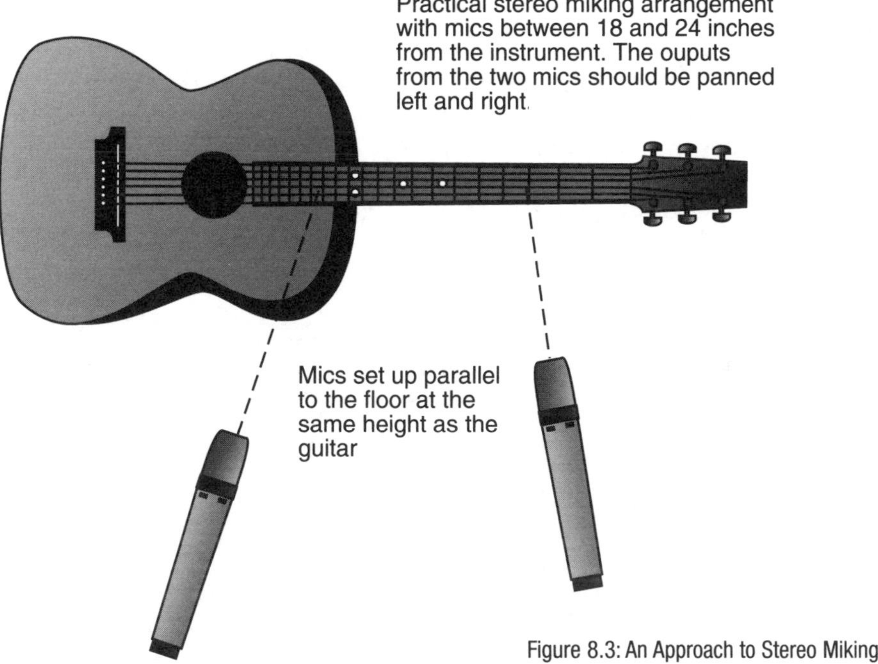

Practical stereo miking arrangement with mics between 18 and 24 inches from the instrument. The ouputs from the two mics should be panned left and right.
Mics set up parallel to the floor at the same height as the guitar

Figure 8.3: An Approach to Stereo Miking

Equalisation

In an ideal world, equalisation would not be necessary, but in the studio, where reality is not always the main objective, some EQ may be necessary. There is no reason to be afraid of using a lot of equalisation as long as you know what you are trying to achieve, but if in doubt, use as little as you can get away with. If the mic positions were correct and the instrument sounded good in the studio, then you shouldn't need to do much to get a good sound, but often, you may have to contend with a less than perfect recording, in which case a little electronic repair work will be necessary.

One of the most persistent problems with acoustic guitar recordings is boominess. This centres around a certain fixed frequency, and you can find out just what this frequency as follows:

★TECHNIQUE

◆ Turn up the boost on your lower mid equaliser and then sweep through the frequency range until the boominess really jumps out at you.

◆ Having found this frequency, which will probably lie between 80Hz and 220Hz, you can bring the boost control back into its cut position, applying just enough cut to tame the resonance.

Top End

◆ General brightening can be achieved using the high equaliser on the mixer to add the required degree of top boost. In circumstances where this is insufficient, don't just go on cranking up the top; all you'll do is bring up the noise and make everything sound harsh. Either re-record the track or use an exciter/enhancer to add a little artificial top end.

◆ Sparkle can be added to the sound by boosting between 5kHz and 10kHz.

◆ Harshness in the upper mid range can usually be reduced by cutting frequencies between 1kHz and 3kHz.

◆ The exact frequency you need to work on is best identified by setting the relevant equaliser section to full boost and then sweeping through the frequency range. When you hit the area you need to boost, it should be obvious. All you need to do then is back off the boost until the sound is as you want it. During this process, keep checking the sound against the EQ bypass position because the ear soon gets acclimatised to radical EQ changes and you may not realise you have gone too far.

◆ In some mixes, you may feel the need to take out all the bottom end to produce a bright, thin rhythm sound. This is common practice and really helps keep the mix sounding clear. The low EQ control may be sufficient to achieve the desired result, but if more cut is needed, try tuning the lower mid control to somewhere between 80Hz and 150Hz and applying more cut with this. It is invariably easier to use EQ cut rather than boost, as there is no danger of overloading the circuitry — with the possible consequence of distortion — and also, the ear is less forgiving of cuts than it is of boost.

Unwanted Noises

Earlier I mentioned the problems caused by string squeaks and over-loud breathing. This can be reduced by the careful use of a parametric equaliser, but accepting that many users don't have these, I have found a way of using the side-chain filters in my gates to achieve the same result. In the Drawmer DS201 gate, as with other models working on a similar principle, the side chain filters are variable frequency, 12dB per octave devices which can be inserted into the audio path simply by selecting the key or side-chain listen mode. This bypasses the gate section and leaves just the filters in series with the input signal as a kind of super equaliser.

The great thing about these filters is that they have a very sharp response, which means that you can take out a high frequency sound without seriously affecting the frequencies directly below. I've had surprising success in filtering both acoustic and electric guitars using these devices, and setting up is quite simple:

★TECHNIQUE

◆ Start off with the high filter in its maximum position.

◆ Now bring it down slowly, while listening to the effect on the recorded sound.

◆ You should find that you can take the edge off the breath and string squeaks without affecting the tone of the guitar too seriously. Of course, if you turn the filter setting down too far, you'll hear the top go from the guitar as well.

◆ For a sharper response, you can put both channels of the gate in series, which will produce a filter response of 24dB per octave if you set the filters to the same frequencies.

Further Processing

Getting the basic guitar sound onto tape and applying a little EQ may be all you need to get exactly the right acoustic guitar sound — on the other hand, it might be just the beginning. There are some engineers who wouldn't dream of recording an acoustic guitar without compressing it at some stage — and it's certainly true that compression does even up the sound a lot. In the case of a strummed rhythm part, compression can smooth out the sound, making it less ragged and more cohesive. By increasing the compressor's attack time to 10mS or so, the attack transients of the guitar remain intact, whereas a short attack time tames the natural attack of the instrument, giving an altogether more consistent sound.

The release time setting of the compressor is also important, because setting it too short can cause the sound to 'pump', especially when a lot of compression has been used. Conversely, setting it too long means that gain reduction may still be applied well after the sound that caused it has fallen back below the threshold resulting in uneven level control. The ideal setting depends on how fast the playing is and on how much pumping can be tolerated, but as a rule, between 250 and 500mS usually does the trick.

Very generally, compressors that sound good on vocals also sound good on acoustic guitars. Soft-knee compressors are normally easier to set up and give consistently decent results, though if you want to juggle the compressor attack time to actually enhance the attack of the instrument, a hard-knee or strict ratio compressor might give you more positive control. By compressing the sound to give a gain reduction of between 6 and 12dB on the loudest sections, it should be possible to even up the sound without inviting too much noise during pauses or quiet sections. If more compression is considered necessary, then consider a compressor with an inbuilt expander gate, or gate the signal before compressing it. Some of the newer compressors also have a built-in enhancer feature to restore brightness lost during heavy compression. Those I've tried work well on acoustic guitar and help maintain an edge to the sound, even when a lot of compression is being used.

Reverb

To achieve a natural guitar sound, it shouldn't be necessary to do much more than add a suitable amount of reverb to the recorded part, and in the case of mono recordings, a stereo reverb can be used to give the sound a sense of space and width which it wouldn't otherwise possess. If the basic sound is sufficiently live but is lacking in width, you could appropriately add a short room reverb or early reflections pattern, which will create a sense of space and identity without making the sound muddy. You might also find that a bright reverb setting will add life to the sound in a way that EQ can't.

★TIP

If a longer reverb is required, don't just solo the guitar and then pick a flattering setting, because you'll find that everything sounds different once the rest of the mix is up and running. Far better to set up a rough mix first and then add the reverb.

★TIP

Rolling some bass off the reverb returns can help to keep the sound clear when a lot of reverb is added, but take care when doing this that the remaining reverb doesn't sound too edgy and thin. There is a tendency to add too much reverb to instruments in a mix, and the professional engineer has come to understand that less is often more. Music relies on contrasts in level, and though reverb does create a sense of space, it also fills the valuable spaces between the notes. On an interesting psychoacoustic note, reverb also creates the illusion of distance, so if you're after an up-front, in-your-face acoustic guitar sound, don't pick a long reverb time. Instead pick a short room, plate or early reflections setting and be sparing in how much you add to the dry signal.

Other Effects

In the context of pop music, a gentle chorus effect works well on the acoustic guitar, giving it an enhanced sense of presence and depth but without making it sound too unnatural or processed. A shallow, mild flange achieves a similar effect — but it isn't always necessary to resort to electronic effects. Take the example of chorus; the effect is designed to create the illusion of two or more instruments playing together, but using multitrack tape, you can do it for real by playing the same part twice on two different tape tracks. If you can't afford the space to leave them on separate tracks, you can always bounce them down onto one afterwards.

★TECHNIQUE

To achieve more of a 'detuned' chorus effect, you could detune the guitar slightly when you do the second take, but a far easier approach is to make use of your tape machine's varispeed control:

◆ Instead of recording one part at the normal speed and one at a slightly altered speed, try recording both parts with the varispeed on — one take with the tape running slightly fast, and the other with it running slightly slow.

◆ When the recording is replayed at the normal speed, this will place the average pitch somewhere between the two, which is more likely to sound in tune with the rest of the track. On the other hand, if you record one part at the normal pitch and then add a second part that is a few cents sharp, the average of the two will still appear slightly sharp.

◆ A shift of less than one per cent in each direction should be sufficient, but do a few trial takes and find what settings give the most appropriate chorus depth. It's also worth noting down the settings for future use.

◆ The two tracks can then be panned to the two sides of the mix, unless you've had to bounce them, in which case a subtle stereo reverb will help recreate the lost sense of space.

◆ It is possible to further exaggerate the chorus effect by delaying one of the guitar parts by a few tens of milliseconds; this is particularly effective if the two tracks can be kept separate for left/right panning. Rather than use a delay unit to create the effect while mixing, it is possible to use a delay unit to delay the headphone feed slightly when recording the second part. In other words, the guitarist is being forced into playing late because he's hearing the backing track after it's been delayed. Figure 8.4 shows this method of delayed monitoring.

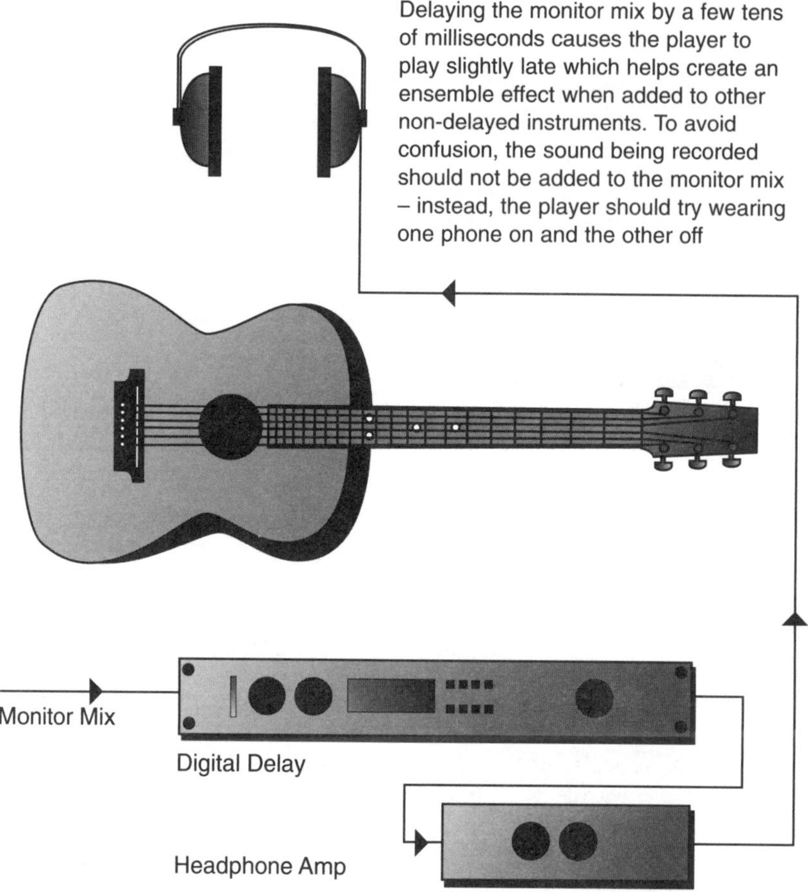

Delaying the monitor mix by a few tens of milliseconds causes the player to play slightly late which helps create an ensemble effect when added to other non-delayed instruments. To avoid confusion, the sound being recorded should not be added to the monitor mix – instead, the player should try wearing one phone on and the other off
Monitor Mix
Digital Delay
Headphone Amp

Figure 8.4: Delaying the Monitoring for Natural Ensemble Effect

If you think about it, this approach is bound to produce better results than using a DDL in the mix because the recorded sound hasn't been processed at all — which means that the quality of the delay line is quite unimportant. Even a budget delay pedal can be used and it won't affect the recording.

chapter 9

electric guitar

The electric guitar sound is the result of a unique symbiosis as, unlike other instruments, it relies on its amplification/loudspeaker system to enhance the sound in a creative way rather than simply to make it louder. Because there are so many different types of guitar and guitar amplifier, and so many playing styles, the range of sounds that can be coaxed from this instrument is vast and varied. The method of recording the instrument adds a further variable, and this potential for creating radically different individual sounds undoubtedly accounts for the continuing popularity of the electric guitar in all forms of contemporary popular music. As the sound is produced via a loudspeaker rather than directly from the instrument, it is useful to examine the guitar amplifier further.

Guitar Amplifiers

Guitar amps are usually fitted with 10 inch or 12 inch speakers, often in multiples, mounted in cabinets which may be sealed or open-backed. The distinctive overdrive sound is caused by harmonic distortion added in the amplifier, but if fed through a full-range monitor speaker system the result is invariably buzzy and unpleasant. Guitar speakers are built with a deliberately poor frequency response, and this has the effect of filtering out the less musical harmonics, resulting in a sound which still has plenty of edge but doesn't sound buzzy or nasty. Furthermore, many guitar speakers are specifically designed to add distortion at high sound levels.

Open-backed cabinets tend to have a fatter sound than closed ones and are often referred to as having a bass thump. That's because the speaker doesn't have a cushion of air to damp it, so low frequency sounds caused by the player's hands hitting the strings cause the speaker cone to move a considerable distance, with an audible thump. This characteristic also affects the more musical sounds of the instrument to quite a large extent, especially on the lower notes. Different players will argue on whether the open- or closed-back cabinet sounds best, but both are quite easy to record.

Most rock guitar players still express a preference for valve amplifiers, as these have a sound quality that is difficult to emulate using solid-state circuitry. Valve circuits, with their transformer output stages, can reproduce transient peaks well in excess of their average rated power handling capacity, while their distortion characteristics when overdriven are considered more 'musical' than those of solid-state designs. The vast majority of guitar amplifiers would be considered technically disastrous from a hi-fi point of view, but the high orders of even harmonic distortion they produce have become synonymous with rock guitar sounds worldwide.

The Guitar

The basic design of the electric guitar has changed little since it was invented — indeed, one of the most popular guitars today is the Fender Stratocaster (or one of its many copies), which was one of the first production electric guitars ever. The electrical principle of the guitar pickup is fairly straightforward and isn't too far removed from the magnetic microphone principle, except that the guitar string takes the place of the diaphragm. The string vibrates within a magnetic field generated by a permanent magnet, causing a signal voltage to be induced in a coil of wire wound around the magnets. It works very well, but as the pickup coil behaves exactly like the coil of a transformer, it also picks up stray magnetic fields from transformers and mains wiring, resulting in a background hum.

Humbuckers

It is possible to cancel out most of the hum by using a pickup with not one but two coils, one wound in the opposite direction to the other. This is the humbucking principle, which was originally devised to cancel the hum generated in loudspeakers in the days when their magnets were energised from the mains current. A well designed humbucker has almost perfect immunity to hum pickup, but because of the different coil impedance and the spaced magnetic pole-pieces, they invariably have a significantly different tonal characteristic than the simple single-coil pickup.

Unfortunately, the guitars that are currently popular tend to feature single-coil pickups, and these can be a nightmare in the studio because nearly every piece of equipment radiates mains hum to some degree. It is possible to rotate the instrument to find a position of least hum, but this imposes restrictions on the player and rarely leads to perfect cancellation. Furthermore, now that computer monitors are commonplace in studios, the problem is worsened, as these radiate a high level of buzz which will interfere with the operation of a single-coil pickup at distances of ten feet or more.

One solution is to use one of the newer mini-humbuckers which come as standard on some instruments and are available as replacements for standard instruments. These locate the two sets of magnets very close together, in an attempt to combine the noise rejection capabilities of a humbucking pickup with the tonal qualities of a single-coil model. Different manufacturers meet the challenge with differing degrees of success, though the better ones come very close indeed.

Active Pickups

Another approach is the so-called active pickup, which usually comprises a low-impedance pickup followed by a battery-powered electronic buffer. These still suffer from interference, though to a lesser extent than a standard pickup, and they offer the advantage that they can be DI'd without the need for a DI matching box if a clean sound is sought. Active models do, however, produce a degree of background noise due to the amplifier circuitry and, when boosted by the extra gain of an overdriven amplifier or effects pedal, the noise level can become obtrusive.

Setting Up

Obviously it is up to the musician to ensure that his or her instrument is properly maintained, but the reality is that many guitar players turn up at the studio with an instrument that is inadequately set up and frequently unrecordable. Professionals are unlikely to fall into this trap, but amateur players coming into the studio for the first time can easily be let down by their instrument. However, there are a few things you can do to help ensure a good result.

◆ Old, worn strings can turn an expensive guitar into an unresponsive, dull and thoroughly uninspiring instrument, so if you know you have a session coming up where the players are inexperienced, ask them to check that their strings are OK, and if not, to replace them a day or two before the recording so as to give them time to settle in. Changing strings directly before a session is merely inviting tuning problems.

◆ Action and intonation problems can defeat the most talented player, and here a little first aid can be administered by an engineer with a little guitar experience. Though this is, again, not the engineer's responsibility, he is inevitably the one who gets the blame when a session goes badly, whatever the true cause. Furthermore, if he can demonstrate an ability to sort out minor problems with guitars and drum kits, he's more likely to win the respect of the artists, which will help the session go more smoothly and possibly win repeat business.

◆ Ideally, the guitar's strings should be as low as possible without buzzing, and the correct neck shape to allow this is not dead straight but slightly concave. If you hold a guitar string down on the first and last frets simultaneously, you should be able to see a small space between the middle of the string and the frets it passes over. If it touches all the way down the neck, it is either too straight, or worse still, a touch convex. Slackening the truss rod an eighth of a turn at a time should correct this problem. A twisted or warped neck will also cause problems with the action of the guitar, but this is beyond the scope of first aid and requires the attention of an experienced guitar technician.

◆ Bad intonation is probably the easiest fault to fix and is caused, mainly, by incorrectly positioned bridge saddles. Using an electronic tuner, compare the pitch of the string fretted at the twelfth fret and the harmonic struck at the same position. If the fretted note is sharper than the harmonic, then the bridge saddle needs to be moved to lengthen the string slightly until the two pitches are the same. Conversely, if the fretted note is flatter than the harmonic, move the bridge saddle slightly towards the neck and try again.

◆ Another less well-known source of intonation error is insufficiently deep nut slots. Aside from making the guitar harder to play, this forces fretted notes to be slightly sharp, as the string is stretched by a small amount when fretted. Owners of such guitars frequently distrust electronic tuners because whenever they tune their open strings, the fretted notes are sharp! Unfortunately, most production guitars suffer from this fault to a greater or lesser extent. A junior hacksaw blade is normally fine enough for deepening nut slots, but only take off a little material at a time, refit the string into the slot, and check the action.

◆ One final tip which can help keep tuning stable is to keep a roll of plumbers' PTFE tape in your spares kit and slide a piece beneath the strings where they cross the nut. The tape will be stretched down into the slots where it acts as a very efficient lubricant to prevent the strings sticking when notes are bent or a tremolo unit used. This is, obviously, unnecessary when using a locking nut system. The tape is thin enough not to affect the action or sustain, but it does help ensure that a bent note returns to its previous pitch when released.

Guitar Noise

Noise is a particular problem with guitars, not just because of the propensity of the pickups to act as aerials for interference, but also because guitar amplifiers tend to be noisy. This isn't down to bad circuit design but is more a function of the tonal voicing of the amplifiers and the high levels of gain needed to produce overdrive sounds. If an attempt is going to be made to remove some of the noise by electronic means, it may be best to leave this until the mixing stage so that an incorrectly set gate or noise filter doesn't ruin a good take.

A dynamic noise filter such as the Symetrix 511A, Drawmer DF320, Rocktron Hush or dbx Silencer can be a powerful ally when cleaning up noisy guitar tracks, and these are generally far more successful than conventional gates. Also known as single-ended noise reduction units, these devices work by reducing the audio bandwidth as the sound level falls; the filter action is so rapid that attack transients pass through with very little change. As any natural sound decays, the higher harmonics decay most rapidly so no significant tonal change is noticed as the filter closes. The filter action is further aided by the fact that electric guitars have a relatively low upper frequency limit anyway — most of their energy is below 3kHz. Because these filters only tackle high frequency noise, many models have an integral expander, which shuts down the audio path once the signal level has fallen below a threshold set by the user.

Noise Filters

Recently, digital noise filtering systems have become available which track the mains frequency and then apply a series of very narrow notch filters to remove both the fundamental and the harmonics that make up the buzz. Because of the precision available with digital filtering, even quite severe buzzes can be removed with little or no subjective effect on the wanted part of the sound.

High frequency hiss is taken care of by means of a multi-band expander which, subjectively, produces similar benefits to those offered by an analogue dynamic filter. At the time of writing, these units are still relatively costly, but in a studio specialising in electric guitar work, they might still be a worthwhile investment.

In the absence of a dynamic filter, a gate may be used to clean up the pauses between notes or phrases, but as electric guitars can sustain for a long time, there may be few periods of true silence where the gate can be effective. In any event, the gate release time needs to be set long enough to allow the guitar to decay naturally without being cut short.

★TIP

Whether you use a gate or a noise filter, it is sensible to use them to process the guitar sound before any delay or reverb effects are added. This way the reverb or delay will decay naturally and will help cover up any slight truncation of the original sound caused by the gate or filter action. Any attempt to filter or gate a sound that contains added reverb is almost certain to change the reverb decay characteristics quite noticeably.

Gate Filters

There is another technique which can be used for cleaning up electric guitar tracks, which relies on the limited bandwidth of guitar amplifiers. Rolling off some EQ above 3kHz should, in theory, remove high-frequency hiss and noise, and allow the guitar sound to pass with little subjective change. In practice, however, the slope characteristics of conventional equalisers restricts their effectiveness in this application because the response is simply not sharp enough. In other words, if the EQ is set to remove the high end noise, the chances are that it will have a significant effect on the wanted sound too.

A solution presents itself in the form of the side-chain filters included in many studio gates, including the popular Drawmer DS201. These are variable frequency filters with a 12dB per octave characteristic designed to process the side-chain input with a view to reducing the risk of false triggering. By selecting the Key Listen mode, it is possible to place these filters in the audio path, enabling the unit to be used as a filter rather than as a gate. And in the fight against noise, the sharp filter response is a powerful ally.

By setting the upper cut-off frequency to between 2.5kHz and 3.5kHz, it is possible to significantly improve the signal-to-noise ratio of a typical electric guitar sound without dulling it noticeably. If an even sharper filter response is required, the two channels of the gate can be wired in series, and with both switched to Key Listen mode, a 24dB per octave filter can be created, simply by setting the upper frequency controls to similar values.

In this application, the sound is usually treated after being recorded to tape, to eliminate the risk of irretrievable overprocessing; the gates are connected to the console via the appropriate channel insert points. As you may have noticed, this technique is very similar to that described in the chapter on Acoustic Guitars for removing finger noise and squeaks; it can also be surprisingly effective at reducing distortion on tape caused by over-recording of clean electric guitar parts.

Microphones

When miking up a guitar amp, it is important to realise that the speaker cabinet should be treated as an instrument in its own right. Much of the sound comes direct from the speakers but there's also a lot of sound emitted from the back and sides of the box, especially in the case of an open-backed cabinet. The sound is different close to the speakers than it is further away in the room, which gives several miking options, including close miking; ambient miking at a distance; and a combined approach with two or more mics set at different distances.

Most British recording engineers choose fairly unsophisticated cardioid, dynamic microphones to record electric guitar, as neither sensitivity nor high frequency extension is a priority, due to the fundamental nature of the electric guitar sound. In other words, guitar amplification systems aren't short on volume and produce very little in the way of true high frequencies.

American engineers, on the other hand, often choose a capacitor microphone for the job, which undoubtedly contributes to the American rock sound. This is not so fat as the English sound and has more top, to the point where a British engineer or producer might consider it too buzzy. A mic with a presence peak will help a sound cut through a mix, but a sound that's already quite abrasive may sound smoother if a fairly flat mic is used. As with vocals, it's down to matching the choice of microphone to the sound you're recording.

Set-Up

To get the sound of a live stack, the textbook approach is to set up a full stack in a big studio, play it loud, and then mic it from several feet with an additional close mic to enhance the bite. The more distant mic captures the direct sound from the speakers plus room reflections, including any phase cancellation effects caused by multiple drivers. Sound is also reflected from the floor, which creates further comb filtering when it arrives at the microphone via different paths.

In other words, the distant mic hears the performance much as an audience would. You can omit the close mic but the sound then tends to be indistinct and distant-sounding, even after considerable EQ'ing.

Close Miking

A more common approach, especially in smaller studios, is to close-mic a smaller amp, such as a single speaker, open-backed combo. The mic is initially positioned very close to the speaker grille and is pointed directly at the centre of the speaker cone. If a less bright sound is sought, it can be moved slightly to one side, which will give a warmer result. Again, an ambient mic may also be used, positioned several feet away. Figure 9.1 shows a guitar combo being recorded via a single microphone.

An even warmer sound may be achieved by miking the rear of the

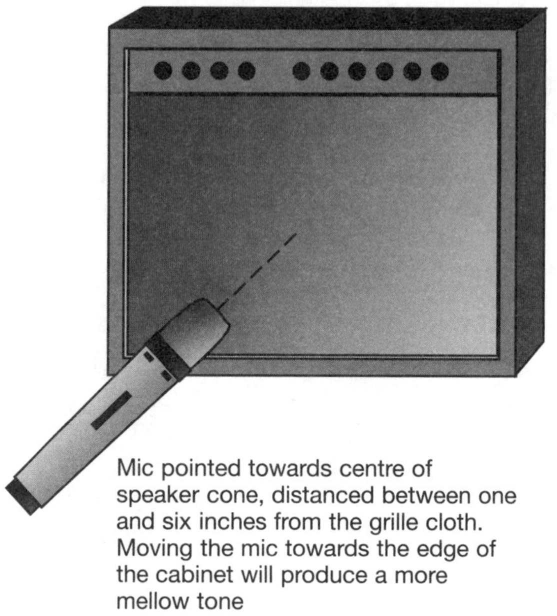

Mic pointed towards centre of speaker cone, distanced between one and six inches from the grille cloth. Moving the mic towards the edge of the cabinet will produce a more mellow tone

Figure 9.1: Close-miking a Guitar Combo

cabinet; indeed, there's no reason not to mic both the front and rear of the cabinet simultaneously if it gives a sound you like. The phase of the rear mic should, strictly speaking, be inverted so that its output is in-phase with that of the front mic, but do try both phase positions, as what is technically correct doesn't always give the best sound.

If you want to try an ambience mic, place it several feet from the cabinet and add this to the close-miked sound, either summed in mono or with one mic panned left and the other right. The ambient mic may be pointed directly at the guitar amplifier or, alternatively, aimed at a reflective surface within the room. Check the sounds individually and you'll soon notice the weighty power of the distant mic compared with the incisive edge of the close-miked sound. For a brighter ambient sound, use a capacitor mic as the distant mic. By combining these two mics in different proportions, a wide range of sounds can be achieved.

If the guitar is played in the control room with the amp itself in the studio, a capacitor microphone may be used to pick up the direct sound from the guitar strings. In isolation, the miked strings will sound very thin, but when mixed in, they will add definition to the notes, rather like an exciter.

★TIP

Again, this is a matter of preference — some engineers and producers use the technique a lot, while others would never bother to do it. A similar effect can be achieved by splitting the guitar output and feeding some of it direct to the console via a DI box.

Processing

Most engineers would agree that adding effects at the mixing stage allows greater creative flexibility, but for a guitarist, the effect may be so much a part of his sound that he can't play the part properly without it. Obviously the right overdrive effect must be set up prior to recording, but effects like chorus, echo and wah wah can also be very important to the performance. Ultimately, the performance is what really counts, so many producers believe that if the player really wants to use his own effects live as he plays, then it's best to let him.

Having put that viewpoint, if some of the effects are too noisy for serious recording and they can't be cleaned up, with dynamic noise filters for example, consider patching them in to allow the player to monitor the desired effects while playing, but record the signal unprocessed. That way you can simulate his effects with high quality studio processors when you come to mix, with the added benefit that the effects can be in stereo, they can be fine-tuned and their level can be changed.

Direct Inject

As an alternative to miking up guitar amplifiers, there's a variety of DI recording techniques available, some of which are very effective and can save a lot of studio time, as well as allowing for greater separation between instruments being recorded simultaneously. It is almost standard practice to DI bass guitars for the majority of pop recording, and even where the amplifier is miked up, some proportion of DI'd sound is often added.

Many players have had bad experiences with DI guitar techniques, to the point that they may even refuse to try them. It's true that they seldom sound exactly the same as a miked-up amplifier, but modern recording preamps and speaker simulators can work exceptionally well. It's true, though, that simply plugging a guitar into an overdrive pedal and the output of the pedal into the desk will produce a disgusting sound.

There are very genuine problems that stand in the way of a good DI'd electric guitar, not the least being that the output impedance of a passive guitar pickup is too high for a mixer's mic or line input. This results in an electrical mismatch, causing loading on the pickups which adversely affects the sustain and tone of the instrument.

Any active DI box will solve the impedance matching problem, but the tone is unlikely to be right. In a guitar amplifier, the frequency response isn't flat but is 'voiced' to sound good; in addition, the guitar speaker completely changes the character of the sound. A basic rhythm sound can be achieved by using a DI box and then applying some corrective or creative EQ, but a dedicated guitar processor will give better results.

Guitar Processors

Direct recording guitar preamps started with the Rockman, which combined compression, delay, chorus, equalisation and overdrive to give a workable clean or dirty guitar sound straight into the mixing desk. The designers appreciated the effect that the speaker has on the overdrive sound and included filtering to simulate this. Though the sound wasn't much like a real miked guitar amp, it was probably the first time a genuinely usable DI'd guitar sound could be obtained.

Since then, many advances have been made, using a variety of technologies. Some designers have chosen to go back to valves in order to capture the authentic tube sound, some have built digital circuits to simulate the same effects, and others employ solid-state, analogue circuitry to do the job.

Many of the newer units are quite sophisticated and offer MIDI-programmable digital multi-effects as well as the more obvious overdrive, EQ and compression. The quality of design has improved over the years and some of the latest units really do come very close to the sound of a miked-up cab. Even so, guitar players always tend to complain that the sound isn't the same as what they hear when standing in front of a loud stack at a gig — though that's hardly surprising, since studios seldom monitor at that kind of level.

The only fair way to judge such a guitar processor is to see if it gives the same kind of sound over the studio monitors that you'd expect to hear from a conventionally miked guitar amp on a record. At the time of writing, the best-sounding recording guitar preamps are those using analogue circuitry to create the overdrive effect, but it is only a matter of time before digital technology beats the problem.

Recording Preamps

Relatively inexpensive recording guitar preamps which have no internal effects and no programmability are available. These are often the most cost-effective way of doing the job, as they are very quick to set up and can be processed via any studio effects unit.

Speaker Emulators

A more basic approach to DI'd guitar is to use a conventional guitar amplifier, but to plug in a speaker simulator instead of the usual speaker. A typical speaker simulator comprises a reactive dummy load, allowing the amplifier to work normally, followed by circuitry that approximates the filtering effect of a guitar loudspeaker. Apart from the dummy load which is, of necessity, passive, the circuitry may either be passive or active and the output appears as either a mic or line level signal that can be plugged directly into a mixing console. Most models can handle up to 100 watts of input power, which means that the majority of guitar amps can be run flat out to get the best overdrive sound. Figure 9.2 shows how a speaker emulator is connected.

Some include switchable filters, enabling them to simulate open- or closed-backed speaker cabinets, and the difference in sound between different models is surprisingly great. As a rule, valve amplifiers produce a nicer overdrive sound when used with speaker simulators than do solid-

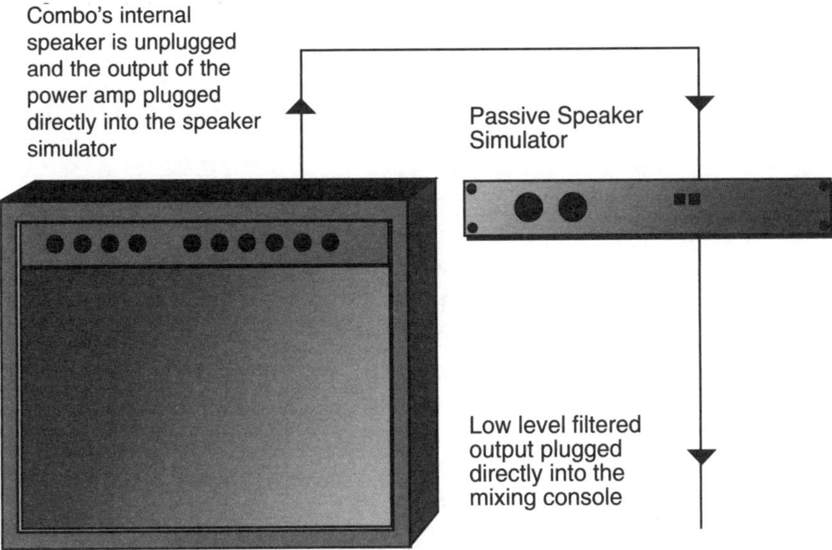

Combo's internal speaker is unplugged and the output of the power amp plugged directly into the speaker simulator
Passive Speaker Simulator
Low level filtered output plugged directly into the mixing console

Figure 9.2 Using a Speaker Emulator

state amplifiers, but in any event, speaker simulators can come very close to the sound of a miked-up amplifier. All that's missing is ambience, which can be applied with a studio reverb processor. Some electronic reverb is an advantage, even if the guitar amp has a built-in spring reverb, because few guitar amplifiers have a stereo output. Adding even a small amount of stereo digital reverb really opens up the sound and creates the impression that it was recorded in a real space.

★TIP

Some engineers have been known to use a guitar sound on tape to drive a guitar amplifier, which is then miked up and re-recorded onto a spare tape track prior to mixing. This means that the original sound can be modified by the character of the amplifier, additional overdrive can be added and different EQ settings tried. It's also possible to mic up the amp in a room with a flattering acoustic which can contribute to the sound. Concrete stairwells, corridors and basements have all been used at one time or another, and the way in which a basic sound can be changed by this method is little short of dramatic.

Equalisation

The electric guitar sound is not natural, so there are no hard and fast rules as to how it should sound. Invariably, some EQ will be necessary to fine-tune the sound and it is quite acceptable to add EQ during recording as well as when mixing. However, don't go overboard with EQ while recording, because few console equalisers are good enough to 'undo' a previous EQ treatment, even if you happen to remember the exact settings used.

Final EQ settings should always be decided in the context of the entire mix — sounds optimised in isolation seldom work properly when everything else is playing. Here are a few guidelines:

◆ Cut applied at between 100Hz and 250Hz can help sort out a boomy or boxy sound; boost in the same range can fatten a thin sound.

◆ Cabinet clunk can be accentuated by boosting at around 75-90Hz, though it can be argued that there's little point adding EQ boost much below 100Hz on a conventional electric guitar, as the fundamental of the lowest note is in the order of 80Hz. All you'll do is bring up the boom of the cabinet or the room resonances which is, generally, not what you want.

◆ Bite can be added to the sound anywhere between 2kHz and 6kHz, depending on the effect you're after. The electric guitar isn't a natural instrument, so the only rule is to get the sound you want. Don't add any really high end boost unless the guitar is DI'd; nothing much over 4kHz comes out of a guitar speaker, so boosting higher than this would simply bring up the background noise for no reason.

◆ Two similar sounding electric guitars can be separated by adding bite at different frequencies — at 3kHz on one guitar and around 4kHz on the other, for example. It also helps to choose two different types of guitar if the parts are both busy — perhaps one single-coil model and one with humbuckers.

◆ Single-coil guitars cut through a mix without taking up too much space, so they may be the best choice in a busy mix. Humbucking pickups create a thicker sound, which can help when aiming for a full sound from a small rock band such as a three-piece lead, bass and drums outfit.

Signal Processing

Aside from optimising the EQ, what else can you do to a guitar sound? The answer to that question really depends on whether you merely wish to enhance the sound or make it significantly different; in extreme cases, the guitar can be so heavily treated that it is no longer recognised as a guitar at all.

Multi-effects processors are relatively cheap, and most allow the user to create reverb, delay, chorus, phasing, flanging, vibrato, pitch shifting and so on; more up-market models offer extras such as panning, exciters, complex equalisers, compressors, gates and auto-wah. The list of possible effects is endless but, as in the worlds of art and music composition, it is often what you leave out that makes more difference than what you put in.

Reverb

If you're after a fairly straight rock sound, then the basic overdrive sound, however achieved, need only be treated with a little EQ and reverb to make it sound right — choosing the right type of reverb is the only problem. For a raunchy, live sound, a short reverb with a fairly bright character is ideal, and the shorter the reverb decay, the more of it you can add into your mix without making the mix sound cluttered. If the original amplifier sound had reverb added, you may even find an early reflection or ambience program works best, as this will add brightness and interest as well as opening up the stereo spread, but without changing the essential character of the original sound too much.

More abstract musical forms may demand a longer, more flowing reverb and these can be combined with repeat multi-echo effects to create a sense of vastness. Further interest can be added by feeding the effects signal through a chorus or flange unit before it gets to the reverb unit. There are no hard and fast rules, but in general terms, the less busy the guitar part, the more reverb you can add before you run into problems. For a more in-depth discussion of the effects of reverb, read the chapter dedicated to reverb treatments.

Compression

Compressors are commonly used on guitar tracks of all types to increase sustain and to keep an even level. In this application, compressors with programme-dependent attack and release times are very helpful, as they will automatically adapt to the different sounds produced by different playing styles. Even a heavily overdriven guitar sound can be made to appear more powerful if compressed, as its average energy level is increased. Of course, manual compressors may also be used, in which case the attack time of the compressor may be increased slightly to give individual notes more attack if desired. Optimum release time depends on playing speed, but around half a second is usually adequate.

Using a faster release time in combination with a high degree of compression can cause audible level pumping, but this artifact may be used creatively to enhance the feeling of power. As a rule, a medium compression ratio of between 3:1 and 5:1 is adequate, with the threshold set to give between 8 and 15dB of gain reduction on the loudest notes.

It must always be borne in mind that 10dB of compression also means a 10dB deterioration in the signal-to-noise ratio during the quieter sections where noise is most likely to be obtrusive, so tracks containing guitar solos are best kept closed down until the moment before their entry. This may be done manually, but is more easily handled by an automated mute system. Remember that guitar amplifiers produce more noise than almost any other instrument (especially during heavy overdrive), which means that special care must be taken if the end recording is not to be compromised.

chapter 10

a universal mic technique

There are well-established microphone techniques for all the more common musical instruments, but the musical world is a large place, and there is an abundance of ethnic instruments for which no standard miking methods exist. Nevertheless, there are a couple of simple rules that can be applied to virtually every instrument ever conceived, and which give acceptable results every time.

Most instruments produce sound from more than one place — take the acoustic guitar; some sound comes out of the sound-hole due to air vibration inside the body, the wooden panels of the body resonate, the strings themselves produce sound, and the neck and headstock vibrate. What we identify as a good acoustic guitar sound is in fact a combination of all these separate sounds. The same is true of all acoustic instruments, and even in the case of an electric instrument such as an amplified guitar, it could be argued that the cabinet vibrates and contributes to the sound directly produced by the loudspeaker.

Mic Distance

Miking distance presents a problem, because if we bring the microphone too close to the instrument, we start to focus on just one part of it, which means that we are no longer capturing the composite sound of the whole instrument. It is tempting to put the microphone close to the part of the instrument that seems to be making the most sound, such as the bell of a trumpet, the sound-hole of a guitar or the head of a drum, and though it is occasionally possible to obtain usable results in this way, what we actually get is not really representative of the whole instrument.

On the other side of the coin, placing the microphone too far away may capture the necessary components of the sound but could also pick up other unwanted sounds or room ambience effects. It is always easier to record an instrument if it is played in a sympathetic acoustic environment, and most western instruments need a little reverberation because they were designed to be played indoors. The same is not necessarily true of ethnic instruments, as many are only ever played out of doors, and thus need a less reflective environment.

Universal Rule

As acoustic instruments vary enormously in loudness and frequency content, I'd tend to choose a capacitor microphone in order to be confident of having a high enough degree of sensitivity and the ability to capture the full audio spectrum. Most instruments sound reasonably accurate to the person playing them, which gives us one fallback position straight away; if all else fails, put a mic close to the player's ears. As I mentioned in an earlier chapter, I've used this technique to good effect when working with acoustic guitars, where a cardioid mic 'looking' over the player's right shoulder will often produce a very natural and well-balanced sound

The other method I've evolved is based on rules normally applied to the stereo miking of ensembles. When working with stereo, it is common practice to create an equilateral triangle with the musicians forming one side of the triangle and the stereo mic array occupying the point opposite. This ensures that all the instruments in the ensemble are roughly the same distance from the mics, yet the mics are close enough to exclude external sounds to a useful degree.

Single Instruments

A typical drum kit is around five feet in width, so a single mic placed five feet in front of the kit will give a usable result. Of course, few people would record the drum kit with a single mic, but it serves to illustrate the principle.

This rule may be extended slightly to accommodate single instruments; it is necessary only to measure the longest dimension of the instrument and then place a cardioid pattern mic at that distance from the instrument and pointing towards its centre. For example, a drum kit is normally miked from between four and five feet, while a piano might be miked at between five and eight feet. This is only a 'rule of thumb', and if it is desirable to capture a little more of the room ambience, then the mic can be moved a little further away until the desired balance is achieved. Even so, check the mic position which results from using this method against the standard mic positions for known instruments and you'll be surprised at how closely they correlate. Virtually all the wind instrument mic positions can be worked out in this way. Likewise, the acoustic guitar can be recorded using a single mic at a distance of around three feet.

The 5:1 Rule

A further consideration arises when several instruments are being recorded together, as it may be necessary to compromise the individual microphone positions in order to minimise leakage or spill between the instruments. Using cardioid pattern mics, it is recommended that the mics be separated by a distance at least five times as great as the distance between the microphones and the instruments they are trained upon. This principle is illustrated in Figure 10.1. A slight improvement in unwanted leakage can be achieved by using a tighter microphone pattern, such as a hypercardioid or supercardioid, but it could also be argued that omnis will produce just as good a result. Admittedly there may be more spill, but because of the improved off-axis response of omni mics, the spill will at least be recorded faithfully.

Cardioids will produce slightly better separation, but their inferior off-axis response means that what spill is picked up may be tonally inaccurate, leading to a less accurate representation of the performance when the outputs from all the mics are mixed. There are cardioids with

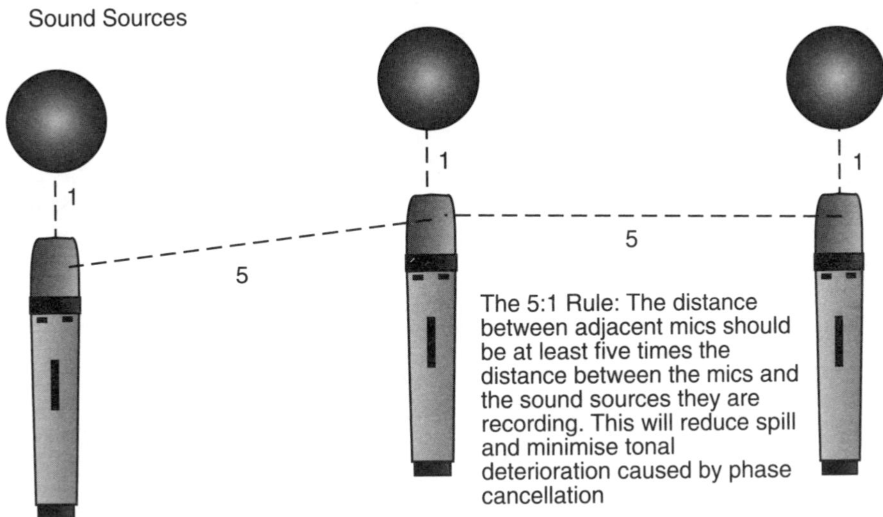

Sound Sources
1
1
1
5
5
The 5:1 Rule: The distance between adjacent mics should be at least five times the distance between the mics and the sound sources they are recording. This will reduce spill and minimise tonal deterioration caused by phase cancellation

Figure 10.1: The 5:1 Rule

excellent off-axis response, but these tend to be rather specialised and very expensive.

Stereo

When attempting stereo recordings of large ensembles, the classic approach is to use a stereo mic pair, usually M&S or XY (coincident) mounted in front of the performers, as stated earlier. In a venue with suitable acoustics, this can produce excellent results, with the outputs from the mics being recorded directly to DAT or a similar stereo recording device. Realistically, though, the balance is unlikely to be exactly right, and although individual performers can be moved around to compensate to some extent, most engineers resort to using spot microphones to reinforce the weaker sections. Working with a small folk duo or string quartet, this may not be a problem, but in situations such as orchestral recording sessions, where much greater microphone distances are involved, the time delay between the sound reaching the spot mics and the main stereo mics becomes significant.

Delay Correction

The time delay problem can be corrected by using a high quality delay line to delay the spot mic outputs by exactly the right amount, so that the signals arriving from both sets of mics are brought back into phase with each other. As sound travels at roughly 300 metres per second, this isn't too difficult to calculate, and the spot mics (suitably panned) can then be added in with the main stereo mics before being recorded onto the stereo machine. Alternatively, the performance can be recorded onto multitrack tape for subsequent mixing. Figure 10.2 shows how the delay is connected.

To do this properly requires a separate digital delay for each spot mic, but in all but the most serious classical recording situations, this might be considered a touch extravagant. It is normally sufficient to delay all the spot mics by the same amount; this is easily achieved by creating a stereo subgroup of the spot mic signals (either while recording or during mixing) and then using a good quality stereo DDL to delay the subgrouped signal by the required amount.

It is essential that the spot mics are panned to the correct positions in the stereo soundstage so that they corroborate the image produced by the main stereo mic array. The delay unit may be connected to the subgroup insert points, and if the business of adding delay can be left until the mixing stage, this gives the added flexibility of being able to 'fine tune' the delay time by ear for the best subjective result.

Esoterica

There is some disagreement as to whether the sound from spot mics should be delayed until it is exactly in phase or whether subjectively better results are produced if the spot mics are slightly over-delayed. The logic behind over-delaying the spot mics is that the sound from them blends in with the early reflections picked up by the main stereo mics.

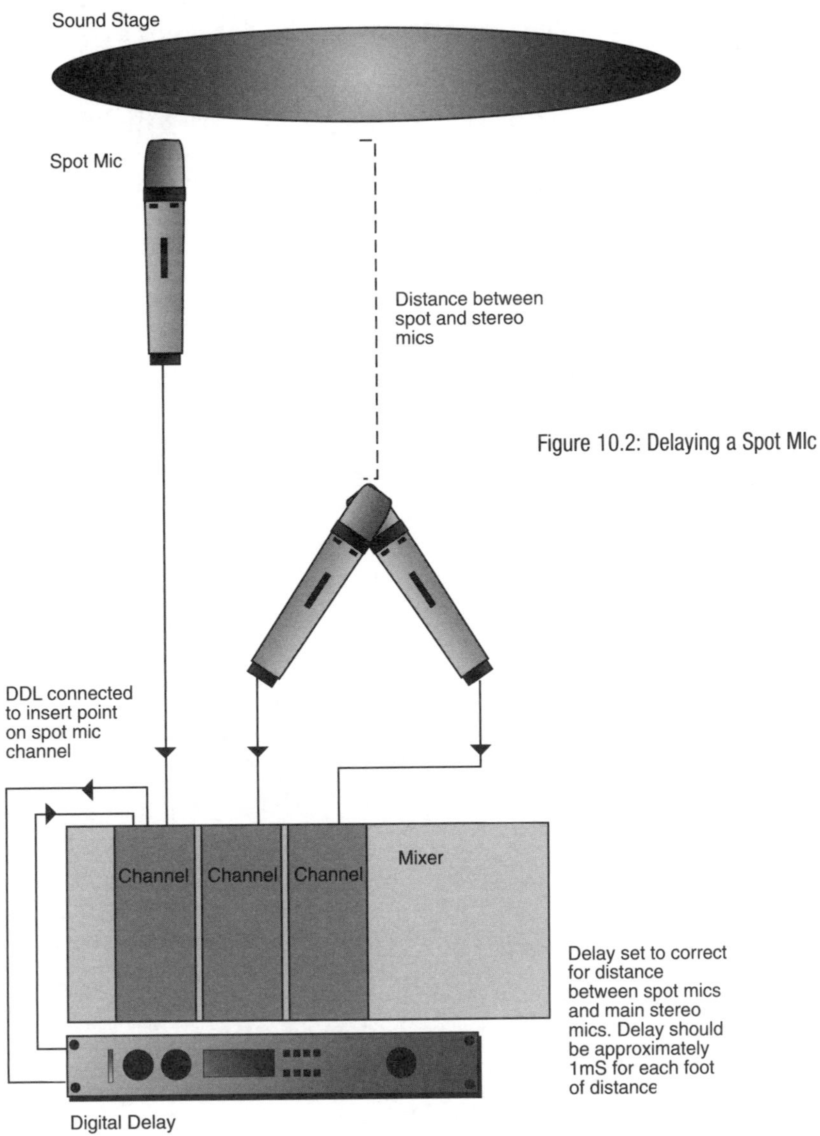

Figure 10.2: Delaying a Spot MIc

This has the effect of changing their subjective level but without the need for the timing to be precisely accurate.

It must be stressed that these are very high-brow considerations and are the subject of debate between engineers at different leading classical record companies. But it strikes me that if a compromise must be made, and all the spot mics have to be processed by a single stereo delay line, over-delaying the sound very slightly, rather than under-delaying it, might achieve a better result — bearing in mind that it is impossible to give all the spot mics exactly the right delay time using a common delay line.

chapter 11

reverb

Reverberation is undoubtedly the most important studio effect at our disposal, and no book on engineering or production would be complete without a section devoted to this subject. In pop music production, and indeed in some classical recording situations, reverberation tends to be added using digital reverberation simulators rather than relying on the natural acoustics of the studio or venue. Digital reverberation units were originally very costly, due to the complexity of their circuitry and the research which went into them, but as new circuit technology was developed and as the principles of artificial reverberation became better established, inexpensive units became commonplace. Nowadays, a basic digital reverberation unit can cost less than a couple of hundred pounds.

The more expensive professional studio reverb units tend to have a better technical specification in terms of noise, audio bandwidth and distortion, and they also produce a more realistic effect. But, though budget units are technically inferior, they still offer surprisingly good reverb simulations and are generally quiet enough, if used with care, to make good master quality recordings. Some models offer a choice of preset reverberation treatments, while others allow every detail of the effect to be programmed. It is, admittedly, useful to be able to vary the more important parameters which make up the reverberation effect, but it is arguable whether the very detailed programming possible on some models is worthwhile. A basic unit offering a choice of over 100 preset reverb treatments (as many now do) will cover most eventualities; such models make ideal second reverb units.

Vital Statistics

When a sound impulse is fed into a reverb unit, there is a short delay before any reverberant sound is heard; this is known as the reverb 'pre-delay', and is often used to increase the impression of room size ,but can also be useful in separating the reverb slightly from the dry sound, especially on vocals, to increase vocal clarity.

Directly after the pre-delay come the so-called 'early reflections', which are really closely spaced, discrete echoes representing the first

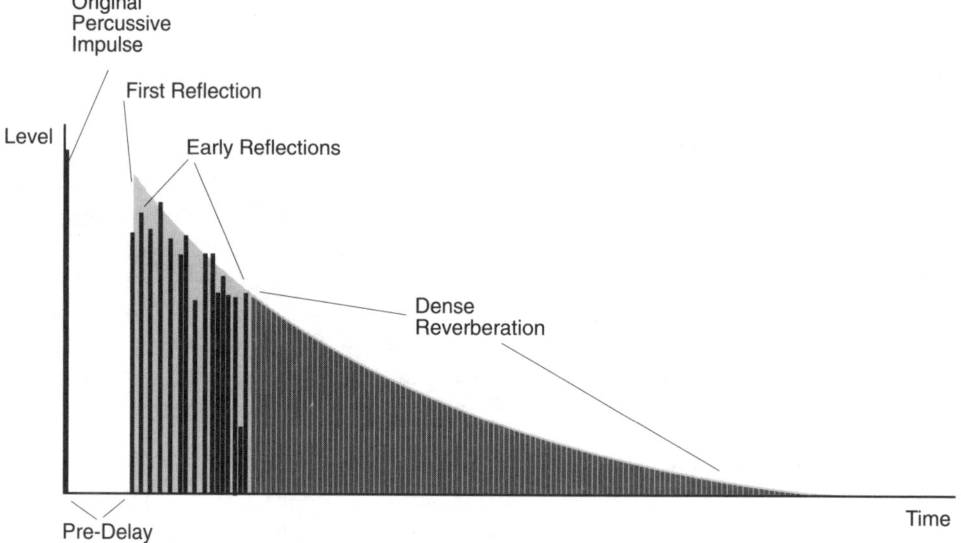

Figure 11.1 Anatomy of Reverberation

reflections from the room boundaries. These discrete reflections quickly build up into a dense, reverberant pattern which further increases in density as its level decays. In a real room, these early reflections help us to localise sounds, and in a digital reverberation simulator, they help create the illusion of space around the sound. Figure 11.1 shows how reverberation develops and decays following a percussive sound.

Early Reflections

Herein lies one major difference between real rooms and artificial reverberators: in a real room, every instrument in an ensemble produces a different early reflection pattern because the performers are occupying different positions relative to the room boundaries. As a consequence, the early reflections from the different instruments tend to blend, creating a more dense, more complex pattern than would be produced if all created the same early reflections pattern.

Artificial reverb devices produce a fixed pattern of early reflections which has the effect of placing every instrument in our imaginary room in the same position. This isn't always a problem, especially when producing pop music, as artistic considerations come before the need for authenticity. But in classical or other 'acoustic' work, it helps to turn down the early reflection level if the reverb unit is programmable, or to pick a hall setting with a slow reverb build-up if the unit offers a choice of presets. Not only does this prevent the 'everything in one place' effect, it also sounds more natural, as most digital reverberation units produce early reflection patterns that are far more obtrusive than those found in real concert halls.

Mono Into Stereo

Reverb units usually take a mono sound source and create a pseudo-stereo output by producing different reverberation patterns for the left and right channels. This is a perfectly viable approach and closely simulates what happens when a single sound source (which can be considered as mono) is heard in a reflective room — different reverberant patterns arrive at the left and right ears of the listener, creating the impression of space. Those units which have stereo inputs invariably sum the two channels to mono for processing, leaving only the dry portion of the sound in stereo. The reverberant sound is generated from the summed mono signal and processed to provide stereo (left and right) outputs. Some units can be programmed to operate as separate mono reverb processors, but these are relatively uncommon.

Real Life

During a real musical performance, all the instruments would normally play in the same room and so be influenced by the same natural acoustic environment. It follows that in order to simulate this using artificial reverberation, all the instruments in the mix should be treated with the same type of reverberation. In the production of pop music, however, we are under no such constraints, as a natural result is not necessarily the most artistically pleasing result. Consequently, it is common practice to use several different reverb settings on the same mix; for example, the vocals might have a medium length, warm-sounding reverb while the snare drum might be treated with a short, bright plate or even a gated setting. Other instruments could be treated with other reverb types or be left completely dry. Furthermore, the relative level of reverb to dry sound is likely to be different in each case. The choice of settings for individual instruments or parts is a purely artistic one, but there are some points to take into consideration which might make this choice more logical.

Psychoacoustics

In nature, reverberation is used by our ears to determine something about our immediate environment. If we hear a sound with a lot of reverberation, we assume that it is quite distant, because nearby sounds will contain far more of the direct portion of the sound and less

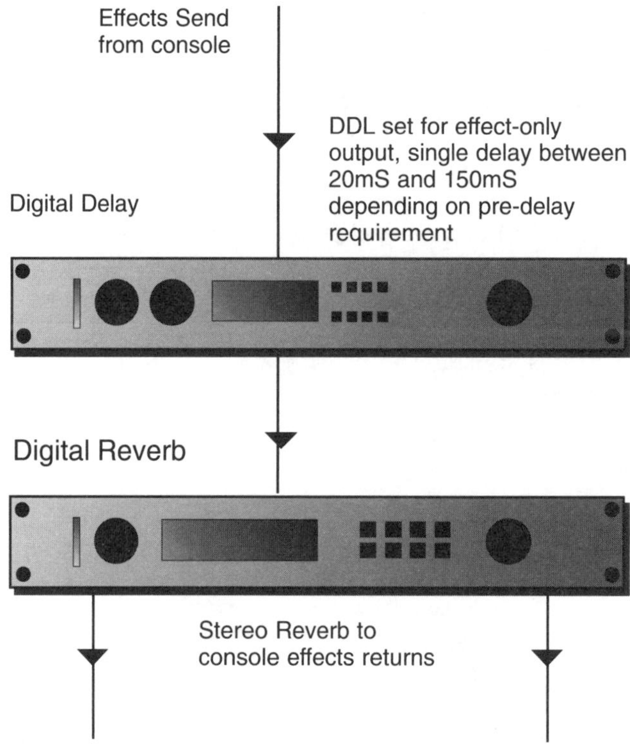

Figure 11.2: Adding Pre-Delay to Reverb

reflected sound. This is true both in and out of doors, though outdoor reverb is only evident in places where there are large reflective surfaces such as buildings, cliffs or densely-growing trees. Furthermore, bright reverbs suggest hard surfaces, while duller or warmer reverbs characterise softer environments such as concert halls.

It can be deduced from these facts that if the level of reverberation following a sound is increased, the sound can be made to seem more distant, and this provides a way of creating a front-to-back perspective in a mix, as opposed to the simple left/right positioning offered by pan pots. Also bear in mind that high frequencies are absorbed by the air, so distant sounds tend to be less bright than nearby sounds.

★TIP

This applies to both the direct and reverberant sound, which means that a sound may be placed in the far distance by using a very high level of reverberant sound with a low level of direct sound and a degree of HF cut. Conversely, the illusion of proximity can be created by placing a relatively bright, dry sound against a backdrop of less bright, more reverberant sounds; this explains why highly reverberant lead vocals need to be mixed at a high level to prevent them receding into the background.

Small Rooms

Small rooms tend to have pronounced early reflection patterns with a fairly rapid reverb decay. Such treatments can be used to create an intimate club atmosphere — it is possible, using very short reverberation decay times, with a relatively high level of reverb compared to the dry sound, to bring a sound alive without making it seem processed in any way at all. That's because we are simulating the type of acoustic that we're used to living and working in — one which we recognise as normal and take for granted. Some reverb units contain specific ambience or early reflections programs, and these are very useful for creating space without apparent reverb. They are also useful for processing tape tracks that have been recorded with a mono effect and which need to be given a sense of width.

★TIP

For example, a vocal recorded with a medium reverb can be processed using an early reflections setting to create the illusion of depth and stereo width. This is extremely useful for 4- and 8-track users who invariably have to bounce tracks together and add some effects as they record.

Further Effects

Reverberation used alone is a very powerful effect, but it can also be combined with delay to make things more interesting.

◆ If you are using a digital reverb with no programmable facilities, you can add pre-delay simply by patching a DDL into the reverb input, using a single repeat at between 30 and 300mS, depending on the effect required. Figure 11.2 shows how this is patched up.

◆ Multi-tapped delays can be used to create very spacious reverb effects, especially if the delay is patched before the reverb unit.

◆ Setting longer, multiple echoes gives a very rich echo effect because each individual echo is surrounded by its own halo of reverb.

◆ Modulating the delay very slightly creates a kind of chorus echo which can work beautifully on guitar or synthesizer.

Multi-effects units don't always allow you to connect the effects in the order you would prefer. This is significant because the order in which effects are connected makes a profound difference to the end result.

Autopanned Reverb

◆ Processing a reverb signal via an autopanner, to sweep it from side to side at a rate of one sweep every couple of seconds or so creates a nice sense of movement without sounding too obvious or gimmicky.

◆ A mono-in/stereo-out autopanner must be fed with a mono reverb signal which can be obtained from the reverb's mono output, if the unit has one, or by combining the two channels using a mixer. Panning this signal from side to side at the rate of half a second or so per sweep creates a distinct side-to-side movement, and if the pan time can be made a multiple of the song tempo, the result can be very subtle. This works particularly well when trying to make backing vocals more interesting or for treating instruments in New Age or ambient music productions.

◆ Alternatively, a stereo panner can be used to treat both the reverb's left and right outputs, causing the left and right signals, in effect, to cross over and back again as the pan progresses.

It is also worth experimenting with processing the send to the reverb unit as follows:

◆ Applying a small pitch detune to the reverb send can thicken the sound, especially if the reverb level is high in the mix; this may be used to good effect on parts such as backing vocals or synthesized strings.

◆ Similarly, applying chorus or mild flange to the reverb input helps add movement and spread to the sound, while the random nature of the reverb breaks up the cyclic nature of the chorus or flange.

Multi-Effects Processors

The hardware required to produce additional studio effects is little different from that used to generate reverb, and in recent years, digital multi-effects units costing little more than straight reverb devices have appeared. Depending on their cost and sophistication, these units may be preset or programmable, and may allow anything from four to 20 effects to be used in combination at the same time. There is usually a limitation to which effects can be used simultaneously and in what order they can be used, the permutations often being grouped into so-called 'algorithms'. These algorithms are, in effect, pre-assigned configurations of effects, where the user can change the parameters of the various effects and store the modified composite effect as a patch for later recall.

Most multi-effects units offer reverb, delay and all the modulated delay effects such as chorus, phasing, flanging and vibrato as standard. More sophisticated models may provide pitch shifting, exciters, compressors, gates and equalisers; guitar-specific models often include overdrive and speaker simulation. These days, it is common practice to use guitar multi-effects units to process synthesizers or samplers to produce overdriven synth guitar sounds or distorted organ simulations.

While the same reverb is often used on several instruments or voices in a mix, this is not really true of complex multiple effects patches. These tend to be created with a specific musical part in mind, are often confined to a single vocal or instrumental part, and may only ever be used in one song.

It is becoming increasingly popular to include real-time MIDI control over key parameters within an effect. This allows a performer to change, for example, reverb decay time or pitch shift amount from a MIDI pedal unit. By the same token, these same parameters may be controlled from a MIDI sequencer, which opens up new avenues for automated effects processing. In this application, some units work better than others — on some the parameter being changed will vary smoothly, while with others, the change can be heard as a series of fine steps. Obviously, the smoother the change, the better.

chapter 12

dynamic control

The term 'dynamic control' is generally held to apply to any automatic process which changes the gain of an audio signal. In the context of outboard equipment, the term refers to compressors and gates, though it could equally cover mixer automation and autopanners. Gates and compressors were originally designed for corrective purposes, but they also have a creative role in the studio, and few modern recordings are made without the help of these devices.

Compressor

A compressor is a device which reduces the dynamic range of an audio signal — in other words, it reduces the difference between the loudest and quietest parts of a piece of music. Compression is invariably necessary when recording vocals, as singers vary in level a great deal, depending on the notes they are singing and on their phrasing. Certain instruments, such as bass, electric and acoustic guitars, also benefit from the use of a compressor to help produce a smooth, even level. The compressor really plays a vital role in pop music production, where dynamics need to be quite strictly controlled, and it also increases the average signal level of a recording — which, when applied to music, helps produce a full and punchy sound. In non-musical applications, such as in the processing of broadcast speech, compression is used to ensure intelligibility at all times.

All conventional compressors work on some form of threshold system and are arranged such that signals exceeding the threshold are processed while those falling below the threshold pass through unchanged. This threshold may be set by the user, either by varying the threshold level relative to the input signal or, conversely, by varying the input signal level relative to a fixed threshold. A further stage of gain, called 'make-up' gain is then provided after processing, to allow the user to restore or 'make up' any gain lost in the processing.

Ratio

When a signal exceeds the threshold set by the user, its level is automatically reduced, the amount depending on the 'ratio' setting. On

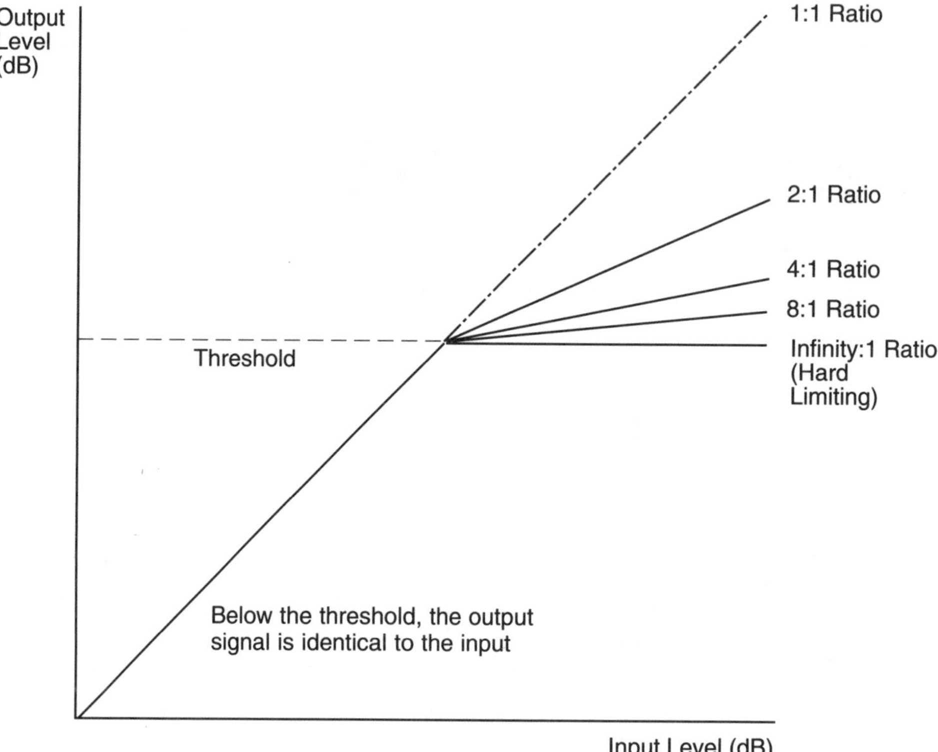

Figure 12.1: Compressor Threshold and Ratio

many compressors, the ratio is variable: the higher the ratio, the more severe the degree of compression. (High ratios produce an effect known as 'limiting', where the input signal is prevented from ever exceeding the threshold.) The best way to understand the effect of a compressor ratio is by giving an example: if a compression ratio of 5:1 is set, an input signal exceeding the threshold by 5dB will cause only a 1dB increase in level at the output. The concept of threshold and ratio is illustrated in the graph in Figure 12.1.

Soft Knee

A standard compressor has a well-defined threshold — if the input signal is just below the threshold, no compression takes place, but if it is just over, then the full compression ratio is applied. An alternative approach is the so-called 'soft-knee' compressor where the threshold level is 'blurred' over a range of 10dB or so. This type of compressor is less able to exercise really

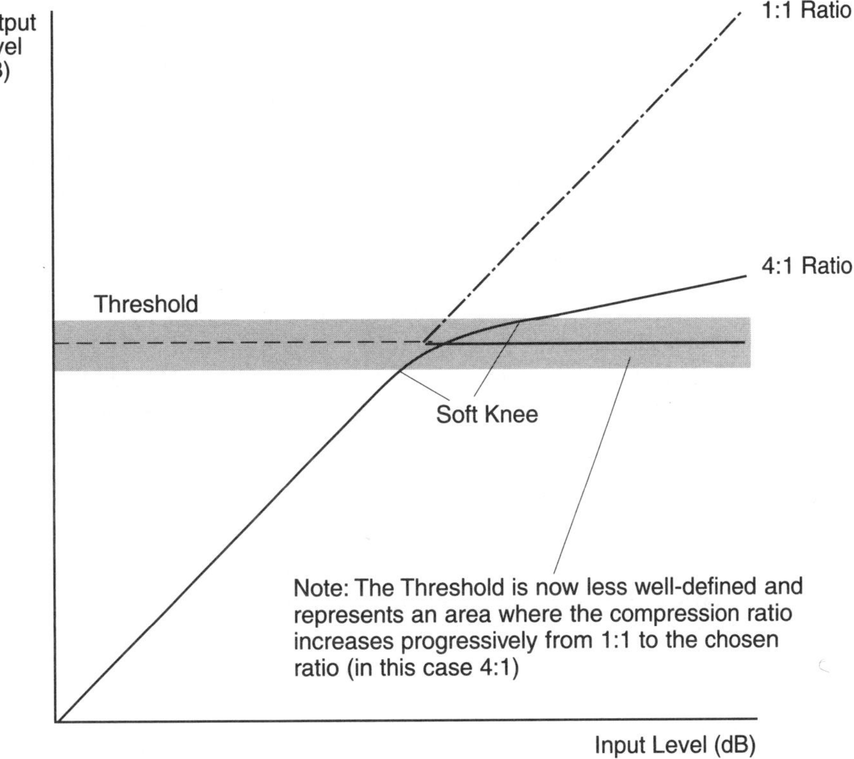

Figure 12.2: Soft Knee Graph

positive gain control than fixed ratio or 'hard-knee' types, but its real advantage is that it is less obtrusive in use, making it suitable for compressing complete mixes or for treating instrumental or vocal sounds that need to retain a natural quality. Figure 12.2 shows how the Soft Knee appears on the Threshold/Ratio graph.

Soft-knee compressors give a more progressive kind of level control, because the compression ratio gradually increases up to the value set by the user rather than being applied abruptly. Hard-knee compressors are better where a more firm degree of control is needed or for making deliberate modifications to the sound of percussive or picked instrumental sounds.

Attack

The term 'attack', in the context of compressors, does not refer to the attack of the sound being processed but to the reaction time of the gain control circuitry within the compressor. The attack time control determines how long the compressor takes to respond once the input signal exceeds the threshold. If the attack is set fast, the signal is brought under control very quickly, whereas a slower attack time might allow the input signal to overshoot the threshold before gain reduction is applied. Allowing deliberate overshoot to occur in this way is a popular method of emphasising the attack characteristics of instruments such as guitars or drums; the slower the attack of the compressor, the more pronounced the attack of the sound being treated.

Release

Release sets the time taken by the compressor to restore the gain to normal once the input signal has fallen back below the threshold. If the release time is set too short, the gain returns to its normal level too quickly, resulting in an audible surge in volume, often referred to as 'gain pumping'. On the other hand, if the release time is set too long, the compressor may still be applying some gain reduction when the next sound comes along — if this is a quiet sound, it will still be suppressed and the benefit of compression will be lost. Long release times can be useful when trying to even out long-term changes in levels, such as the differences in level of different songs on a radio broadcast. However, in music mixing applications, a typical release time is in the order of half a second.

Auto Mode

Optimising the attack and release settings of a compressor is not difficult when the dynamics of the signal being processed are consistent, but if the dynamics are consistently varying, as is the case with most complete mixes, slap bass parts and some vocal lines, then the ideal settings are less obvious. In such situations, it is often better to use a compressor which has an auto attack/release feature. When the auto mode is selected, the compressor analyses the dynamics of the incoming signal and varies its attack and release times 'on the fly' to maintain maximum control with the minimum of side effects. For complex mixes or signals with varying or unpredictable dynamics, the auto setting is usually most effective.

Problems With Compressors

Compressors are not without their negative aspects. For every dB of compression we apply, we also bring up the background noise by 1dB. This might not be obvious at first because, as I've said, a compressor only affects signals exceeding its threshold, and even then, it turns the sound level down, not up. However, the reason for the increase in noise is obvious if you think about it. If we use a compressor to reduce the highest signal peaks by, say, 10dB, we're likely to use the make-up gain control to restore the peak level of the signal to its original value. This means applying 10dB of gain to the whole signal, with the result that any noise present in the signal will also be boosted by 10dB. This will be most apparent when there is no wanted signal to hide the noise, as is the case with low level signals that don't exceed the threshold.

Excessive noise can be alleviated to some extent by using a gate or expander before the compressor, to ensure that breaks and pauses are completely silent; many compressors now come with an inbuilt expander for this very reason. However, this is a corrective measure and, as such, is less satisfactory than the preventative measure of ensuring that the original signal is as free of noise as is possible. In practice, an expander used to clean up a well-recorded signal with a low noise content produces very good results.

Where And When

Most engineers tend to compress their signals while recording and then again during mixing. There are good reasons for this, the main one being that compressing a signal while recording it makes the best use of the tape's dynamic range and, at the same time, helps to prevent unexpected signal peaks from overloading the tape machine. Because any processing applied during recording is irreversible, it is normal to use rather less compression than might ultimately be needed, so that a little more can be added at the mixing stage if required. It is at this latter stage that the expander or gate is best applied to clean up the pauses. If the gate setting is incorrect, the tape can always be run again, but if a mistake is made during recording, an otherwise perfect take may be ruined.

Compressor Sound

Much of what I've explained so far is common knowledge in recording circles, but what may be less obvious is why different models of compressor can sound so different to each other. Part of the difference can be attributed to the side-chain detector circuit — that part of the system which analyses the dynamics of the incoming signal. There are two distinct types in use: peak detecting and RMS detecting. A peak detecting circuit, as its name suggests, will respond to peaks in the input signal regardless of how short they are, while the RMS detector averages the signal level over a short period of time.

The latter approach is more akin to the workings of the human ear and so tends to give a more natural type of dynamic control, but it has a disadvantage in that short signal peaks can get through undetected. Of course, short peaks may also get through any type of compressor unchecked, unless the fastest attack time is set, which is why, in some critical applications, a fast peak limiter is also required. A good example of this is digital recording, where signals larger than the maximum permitted level must be avoided, or serious audible distortion will result. It is possible to patch a separate limiter after the compressor, but in critical applications such as digital mastering or broadcast, it may be desirable to use a compressor with a built-in peak limiter.

The limiter threshold is invariably set higher than the compressor threshold and such limiters are very fast acting, thus preventing any overshoot. In practice, most employ a clipping circuit which physically arrests any signal trying to exceed the limiter threshold until the necessary gain correction has been applied. Though this kind of limiter action is pretty drastic, the sound it produces can be useful in a creative way, especially on rock music.

Side-Effects

Most of the energy in a typical music signal resides in the lower frequencies, which means that the bass drum, bass guitar and, to a lesser extent, the snare drum control most of what the compressor is doing. This shows up one real weakness of compressors, which is that any high frequency sounds occurring at the same time as a low frequency sound will be turned down as the compressor responds to the input signal level. For example, a quiet hi-hat beat occurring at the same time as a bass drum beat will be reduced in level even though it isn't too loud. The usual way around this is to set a longer attack time on the compressor to allow the attack of the beat to get through unchecked; even so, if a lot of compression is applied to a complex mix, the sound can become dull as the high frequency detail is overruled by the low frequency peaks .

Some of the early valve compressors seemed to suffer less from this problem than apparently more sophisticated later designs, and here's one of the reasons — most valve compressors introduce a significant amount of even harmonic distortion, which increases as gain reduction is applied. This has the effect of brightening the sound, very much like an exciter, which helps to compensate for the over-reduction in level of high frequencies. A little even-order harmonic distortion can actually make a signal sound brighter and cleaner than it really is — and valve compressors were adding this distortion quite unintentionally.

Some early FET-based designs also introduced a similar kind of distortion, which is why FET compressors can sound very similar to valve models. More recent designs have attempted to recreate this serendipitous combination of effects by building in a degree of harmonic distortion or dynamic equalisation, which provides a subtle treble boost related to the amount of gain reduction taking place. This can work very well in maintaining a detailed and relatively transparent sound, even when heavy compression is taking place.

Ducking

Though compressors are used, in the main, to smooth out large fluctuations in signal level, they may also be used to allow one signal to control the level of another. This technique is generally referred to as ducking and is frequently used by radio DJs to allow the level of background music to be controlled by the level of the voice-over. As the DJ starts to speak, the level of the background music drops, but whenever there is a pause in the speech, the background music will return to its normal level, at a rate determined by the setting of the compressor's release control.

Such techniques are only possible if the compressor being used has side-chain access. Normally the side-chain of a compressor is fed from its own input signal, but if it is fed from an external source instead, the dynamics of that external source will control the gain reduction process. In our DJ example, if music is fed into the main compressor input and the DJ's voice is fed into the side-chain or external input, whenever the DJ's voice exceeds the threshold level, gain reduction will be applied to the music. The amount of gain reduction will depend on the compression ratio that has been set; many engineers prefer to use a gate with a dedicated ducking facility in preference to a compressor because the results are more predictable.

Apart from the obvious application just described, ducking can be very useful when mixing pop or rock music.

★TIP

Loud, relentless rhythm guitar or pad keyboard parts can be forced down in level to allow the vocals to punch through. The amount of ducking needed to make this work is surprisingly small — a drop in level of just 2 or 3dB is often sufficient to avoid conflict, and the slight gain pumping effect caused by the gain change can add to the sense of power. It is important not to overdo the effect, though, as once the gain changes start to become noticeable, they cease to be pleasant.

Apart from controlling one instrument level with a voice or other instrument (such as solo guitar), ducking may also be used to control the output level from an effects unit. Reverb or delay are very powerful effects, but if too much is used in a busy mix, the result can be very cluttered. Nevertheless, the same mix might have sudden breaks or stops where a high level of reverb or delay is necessary.

★TIP

The answer is to use, say, the drum part to feed the external side-chain input of the compressor and feed the reverb or delay outputs through the compressor's main input. Now, whenever the drums stop, the effect level will return to normal, but when the drums are playing, ducking will take place and the level of the effect will be reduced. Figure 12.3 shows how a ducker might be used in the context of using a voice-over to control the level of background music.

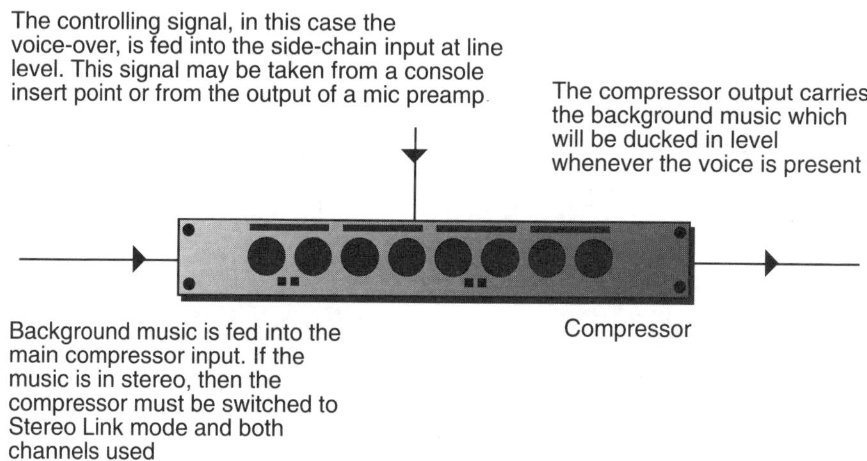

The controlling signal, in this case the voice-over, is fed into the side-chain input at line level. This signal may be taken from a console insert point or from the output of a mic preamp.
The compressor output carries the background music which will be ducked in level whenever the voice is present
Background music is fed into the main compressor input. If the music is in stereo, then the compressor must be switched to Stereo Link mode and both channels used
Compressor
Note: The compressor Attack time determines how quickly the compressor will react when the voice signal is present. The compressor Release time determines how long the background music takes to rise back to its normal level once the voice stops

Figure 12.3: Using a Compressor as a Ducker

Compressor Distortion

We have already touched upon valve and FET distortion, which can work to our advantage by brightening heavily compressed sounds, but there are other, less pleasant distortion mechanisms to be aware of. Normally, a compressor's side-chain follows the envelope of the signal being fed into it, but if the attack and release times are set to their fastest positions, it is possible that the compressor will attempt to respond not to the envelope of the input signal but to individual cycles of the input waveform.

This is particularly significant when the input signal is from a bass instrument, as the individual cycles are relatively long. If tracking of the individual waveform cycles is allowed to occur, very bad distortion is audible

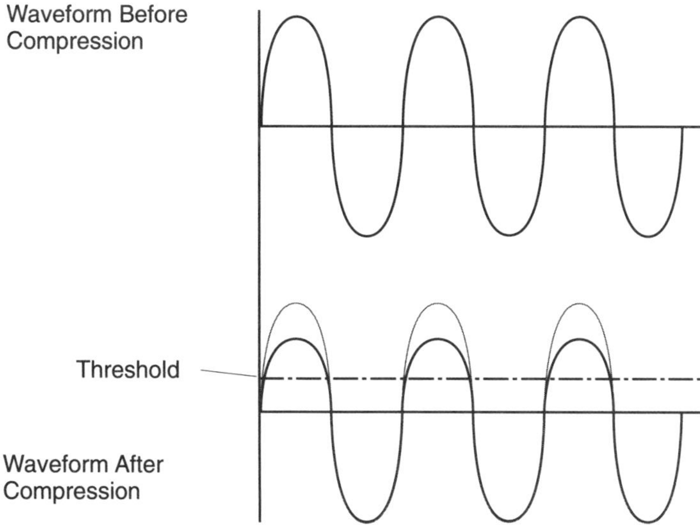

Note how the positive half of the wave is 'squashed' as it exceeds the threshold level. This problem is most evident on low frequency sounds such as bass instruments and oly happens when very fast attack and release times are used on a compressor that doesn't have a hold facility. Some designs have a built-in hold time which is invisible to the user.

Figure 12.4: Compressor Distortion

as the cycles are compressed 'out of shape'. The way to get around the problem is either to increase the release time of the compressor or, if your model allows it, increase the compressor's hold time. The hold facility is a simple time delay that prevents the compressor from going into its release cycle until a certain time has elapsed after the input signal has fallen below the threshold. If the hold time is set longer than the lowest audio frequency likely to be encountered, the compressor will never be able to release quickly enough to distort individual cycles. A hold time of around 50mS should cover all eventualities, and some manufacturers build a fixed hold time of this order into their compressors to make them, in effect, undistortable. Such a short hold time is unlikely to restrict the flexibility of the compressor in any way and there is a very good argument for including a fixed hold time of around 50mS in all compressor designs. Figure 12.4 illustrates the effect of compressor distortion when fast attack and release times are used with no hold time.

De-Essing

A typical compressor reacts equally to all input signals, whether they are bass sounds or high-pitched instruments. For routine gain reduction applications, this is exactly what is required, but sometimes it is desirable to have the compressor react more strongly to some frequencies than to others. The prime example is in de-essing, where we need to remove or reduce the sibilant content of a vocal signal. Sibilance is caused by breath passing around the lips and teeth of the singer and manifests itself as a very high-pitched whistle which can be very distracting and is further exacerbated by high frequency EQ, heavy compression or digital reverberation.

★TECHNIQUE

◆ If an equaliser is inserted into the side-chain signal path of a compressor, the equaliser can be used to determine which section of the audio spectrum is compressed the most.

◆ Sibilance normally occurs in the 5 to 10kHz region of the audio spectrum, so if the equaliser is tuned to the offending frequency and set to give, say 10dB of boost, then compression will occur at this frequency at a level 10dB lower than the rest of the audio spectrum.

◆ Both graphic and parametric equalisers can be used in this application, the parametric giving more control. The equaliser can be set up by listening to the equaliser output and then tuning the frequency control until the sibilant part of the input signal is most pronounced.

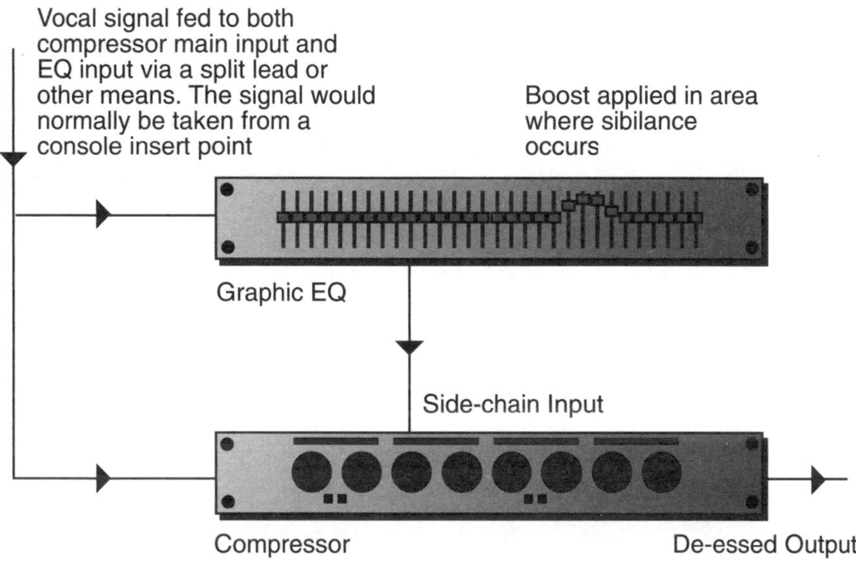
Vocal signal fed to both compressor main input and EQ input via a split lead or other means. The signal would normally be taken from a console insert point
Boost applied in area where sibilance occurs
Graphic EQ
Side-chain Input
Compressor
De-essed Output

Figure 12.5: De-essing with a Compressor

◆ By careful setting of the threshold and ratio controls, the sibilant sounds can be pushed down in level quite dramatically without significantly affecting the wanted sounds. However, if the amount of processing is too high, there will be a noticeable drop in gain whenever a sibilant sound occurs and this can be almost as annoying as the sibilance itself. Figure 12.5 shows how a conventional compressor may be used as a de-esser.

Dedicated De-Essers

A better approach is to use one of the more sophisticated, dedicated de-essers. Using a compressor as above results in the gain of the whole signal being reduced whenever a sibilant sound occurs. Ideally, we would reduce only the level of those frequencies that make up sibilance. Some of the more refined, dedicated de-essers do just this by using either a shelf or notch filter to reduce the gain in the 5-10kHz region whenever a sibilant sound is detected. This allows more processing to be applied without any undesirable side-effects becoming noticeable. Prevention is, however, far better than cure, and if using a different microphone or changing the microphone position can help reduce the sibilance at source, this should be done.

chapter 13

gates and expanders

Gates were first devised to solve a problem in the film industry, where dialogue was often recorded under less than ideal conditions due to the need to keep the microphone out of shot. Their purpose is to shut down the signal path when the signal falls below a threshold set by the user; normally, this threshold will be set just above the ambient noise floor. When the gate is open, both the wanted signal and the unwanted noise pass through, the noise (hopefully) being masked by the signal. During pauses in the wanted signal the gate closes, and in doing so shuts off the background noise which would otherwise be clearly audible in the absence of any signal large enough to mask it.

Gates have undergone a process of refinement over the past couple of decades, and modern models can be quite sophisticated. Like the compressor, they now have attack and release controls which determine how quickly they respond, enabling them to be used to process most types of sound without undue difficulty. The fastest attack settings are used to allow percussive or highly transient sounds to pass through cleanly, while slower attack settings enable the gate to open more smoothly when processing signals which themselves have longer attack times, such as bowed strings.

The variable release time of a gate is also vital in that it enables the gate to close gradually when sounds with a slow decay are being processed. Examples of such sounds are plucked strings, some synthesized sounds, and sounds that have a long reverberant 'tail'. As with the compressor, problems can arise if the fastest attack and release times are set, as the gate triggers on each individual cycle of the input, producing a badly distorted, gritty sound. The solution is the same as for the compressor — many newer gates have a hold feature or a built-in hold time. In the absence of a hold facility, it is necessary to extend the release time until the problem disappears. The envelope structure of a typical gate is shown in Figure 13.1.

★TECHNIQUE

The hold facility may also be used in a creative way to produce hard 'gated' reverb or ambience sounds. If the reverberant sound is fed into the

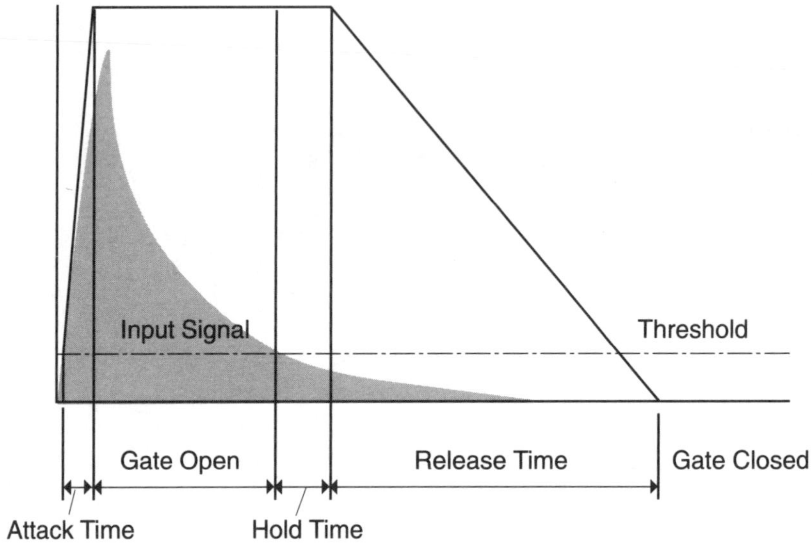

Figure 13.1: Typical Gate Envelope.

gate and then triggered externally using a mic located close to the drum, the gate can be used to impose an envelope on the reverberant sound. A fast release time combined with half a second or so of hold time produces the familiar gated drum sound when used to treat percussion.

Side-Chain Filters

A feature which is common on newer gates is side-chain filtering. This usually takes the form of a pair of shelving equalisers, one high-pass and one low-pass, connected in series with the side-chain circuitry. By varying the filter settings, it is possible to make the gate respond only to a selected band of frequencies, which helps exclude unwanted sounds in situations where spill is likely to cause false triggering. An example of a situation in which filters can be helpful is when miking a drum kit, where sounds from all the drums spill into all the mics to a greater or lesser extent. By making the gate selective, it is possible to reduce the risk of, say, the hi-hat triggering the snare gate.

★TIP

By setting the filters to minimise the amount of hi-hat spill fed to the side-chain, while at the same time maximising the amount of snare signal, a greater degree of separation can be obtained. This can only be achieved by listening to the filter output while adjusting the controls when 'key listen' is selected during setting up. It is important to realise that the filters are only connected in series with the side-chain signal path and do not affect the main input in any way. The only exception to this rule is when the filters are deliberately used as an equaliser by leaving the gate set to the 'key listen' mode.

Gating While Mixing

Gates are very important in multitrack recording, even when the recordings appear to be relatively free of noise. In a multitrack situation, the noise from all the tracks adds up cumulatively, so if a track can be gated into silence when nothing is playing, the finished mix can be made considerably cleaner. For example, the vocalist will not be singing during instrumental breaks and solos, so it makes sense to gate the vocal track in order to mute any tape noise from that track, as well as breath noise and any spill from the headphones that might otherwise be audible during pauses in the singing.

It is also desirable to gate electric guitars, as they have a relatively poor noise performance, especially when used for overdriven or heavily distorted lead guitar sounds. Using a gate will remove the hum, hiss and buzz generated by a guitar amplifier, and can significantly improve the clarity of the final recording.

Gating is best carried out after the signal has been recorded rather than during recording, for the obvious reason that an incorrectly set gate at the recording stage can ruin a take beyond any hope of salvage. Nevertheless, sometimes it is necessary to gate while recording — for example, in situations where several signals have to be mixed onto one tape track and only one of these is to be gated. In this instance, it is wise to set the gate attenuation control to give only as much attenuation as is really necessary and to err on the side of caution when setting the threshold. It is better to put up with a little unwanted spill than to suffer a signal with vital sections cut out of it by an overzealous gate!

Alternative Filter Applications

The side-chain filters used in gates necessarily have a very sharp response — usually 12dB per octave. This makes them far more selective than most conventional equalisers, and in some circumstances, the filters in a spare gate can be used to supplement the basic desk EQ. To do this it is only necessary to leave the gate switched to 'side-chain listen'; the gate will be bypassed and the filters placed in-line with the signal path.

★TIP

The low-pass filter can work wonders in removing high frequency noise from an electric guitar track without significantly changing the character of the basic guitar sound, while the high-pass filter can be used to remove low frequency hums and rumbles as well as to 'thin out' rhythm guitar or backing vocal parts. In very desperate circumstances, the low-pass filter can even be used to reduce the effects of overload distortion on recordings of rhythm guitar and other dynamic sounds, where a little too much enthusiasm on the part of the player can drive the tape machine or mixing console into clipping.

External Control

Gates can be externally triggered via their side-chain access points, allowing the level of one signal to be controlled by another. An 'External' switch is usually provided to enable the side-chain input, though some models may simply be fitted with a side-chain access jack wired in the same way as a console insert point. Used normally, this facility enables the signal routed through the gate to be turned on and off by the signal fed into the side chain. For example:

★TIP

• A sustained sound fed through the gate could be turned on and off by a drum beat fed into the side-chain input. The rate at which it turns on and off depends on the attack and release settings, but it does provide a novel way to synchronise a sustained sound with a percussive one. Figure 13.2 shows how this might be set up.

◆ Bass synth sounds can be gated so that they appear only when a bass drum is present.

◆ Synthesizer chords can be gated from a rhythm pattern to create a synchronised arpeggio effect.

◆ A popular trick is to use the bass drum in a track to trigger the gate while passing the bass guitar track through the gate. The attenuation range control may then be set to reduce or even remove any bass guitar notes not falling directly on top of bass drum beats which can help to tighten up an otherwise sloppy track. The gate release time control is set to allow the bass guitar notes to decay at an appropriate rate.

Gate Ducking

If the gate has a Duck facility, it can be used as a ducker in exactly the

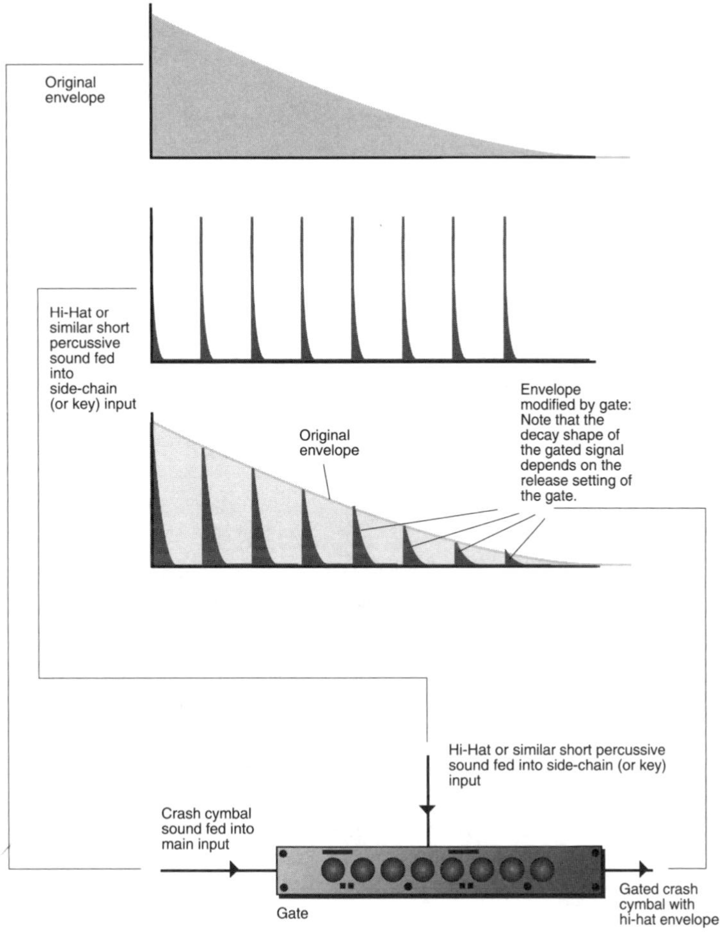

Figure 13.2: Gating a Slowly Decaying Sound with a Percussive Sound

same way as a compressor. The attenuation control of the gate can be used to determine how much the signal level drops once the side-chain input signal (a voice, for example) exceeds the threshold, and as this control is calibrated directly in dBs, it is much easier to set up a precise ducking effect using one of these gates than it is using a compressor. Again, the gate's attack and release times determine how fast the ducked signal will fade out and in again in response to the side-chain input.

Gate Panning

The side-chain access facility of a gate also means it can be used to produce a limited range of panning effects.

★TECHNIQUE

◆ If the signal to be panned is fed into both channels of a two-channel gate, the side-chain inputs could alternately be fed with percussive sounds from a drum machine.

◆ By setting the attack and release times of the gate to fairly long values and panning the two outputs hard left and right in the mix, the signal will appear to move back and forth between the speakers as first one channel is triggered and then the other. Figure 13.3 shows how this is done.

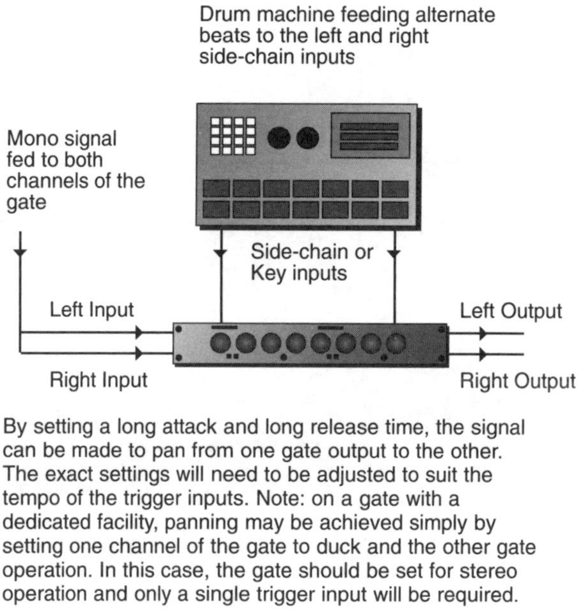

Drum machine feeding alternate beats to the left and right side-chain inputs

Mono signal fed to both channels of the gate

Side-chain or Key inputs

Left Input

Right Input

Left Output

Right Output

By setting a long attack and long release time, the signal can be made to pan from one gate output to the other. The exact settings will need to be adjusted to suit the tempo of the trigger inputs. Note: on a gate with a dedicated facility, panning may be achieved simply by setting one channel of the gate to duck and the other gate operation. In this case, the gate should be set for stereo operation and only a single trigger input will be required.

Figure 13.3 Panning with a Gate

◆ If the gate has a ducking function, the process is simplified further; one channel is set to gate, the other to duck, and the two channels linked for stereo operation. Now feeding a single pulse or drum sound into one side-chain input will cause the signal to pan and then return.

◆ If the tempo of the drum machine is synchronised to that of the music by means of a tape time code track or similar, the pan timing is accurately synchronised to the tempo of the music. Furthermore, the pan triggers don't have to be evenly spaced but can follow a suitable rhythm, allowing more complex effects to be created.

◆ This basic triggered pan set-up can be further modified to produce a passable rotary speaker simulation, simply by feeding the two gate outputs into two equalisers, each set to give a noticeably different sound as shown in Figure 13.4.

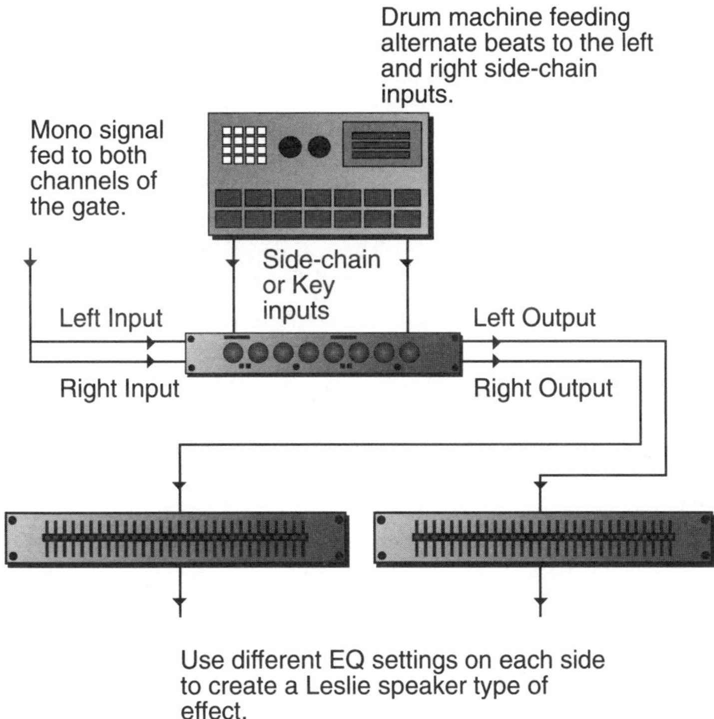

Figure 13.4: Leslie Simulation using Panned EQ

Expanders

Though they perform a similar task to gates, expanders are easier to understand if you think of them as compressors in reverse. Compressors reduce the gain of a signal once it exceeds the threshold, while expanders apply gain reduction to signals falling below the threshold. Whereas a gate will close completely when the signal falls below its threshold, the expander reduces the gain of below-threshold signals by a user-definable ratio, just like the compressor. For example, if the expansion ratio is set to 1:2, for every

1dB the signal falls below the threshold, the output will fall by 2dB. This produces a more progressive and more subtle muting effect than can be achieved using gates, but because the action of a gate is smoothed considerably by its attack and release controls, both gates and expanders behave in a subjectively very similar way when used to clean up sounds. The smaller the expansion ratio, the more subtle the gain reduction effect; a high expansion ratio will make the expander behave in exactly the same way as a gate. Expanders are often incorporated into compressor designs because they are less critical to set up than gates, yet still provide a worthwhile reduction in noise during pauses in the signal.

chapter 14

minimum signal path

In the studio, we rely on the mixing desk and patchbay to such an extent that we often forget about alternative methods of routing signals to tape while recording. In this era of high quality digital or analogue/Dolby S recording, engineers are becoming more quality conscious, and in some circumstances, passing an electrical signal through an entire mixing console just to get it onto tape isn't the best way to do the job. No matter how well the mixer is designed, some signal degradation must take place, and the more circuitry the signal has to pass through, the worse the degradation will be. Take the example of a single microphone signal that needs to be amplified and then routed to a single track on the tape machine: sending it through the console might be the easiest method, but it certainly isn't the best in terms of quality. Think about all the circuitry, switches and controls in a typical mixer channel, and then add that to the routing switches and the group output electronics; it's hardly surprising that the signal suffers.

Mic Preamps

A more purist approach to recording vocals is to use a separate, high quality microphone preamplifier plugged directly into the tape machine. This is known as the 'minimum signal path' approach, and the more discerning engineer may choose to record important parts such as lead vocals in exactly this way. If the vocal needs compressing on the way to tape, a compressor may be patched between the mic amp and tape machine, or a compressor with a built-in mic amp may be used instead. Aside from avoiding unnecessary circuitry in the mixer itself, it is possible to bypass the patchbay too by plugging directly into the back of the tape machine. Although patchbays contain no active circuitry, contact corrosion and dirt can add considerably to the noise and distortion present in a signal passing through the patchbay. Figure 14.1 shows a practical approach to recording vocals without going via the mixing console.

DI Boxes

Line level signals can also be recorded direct to tape, preferably via a DI box, which will match the impedance of the source to that of the tape

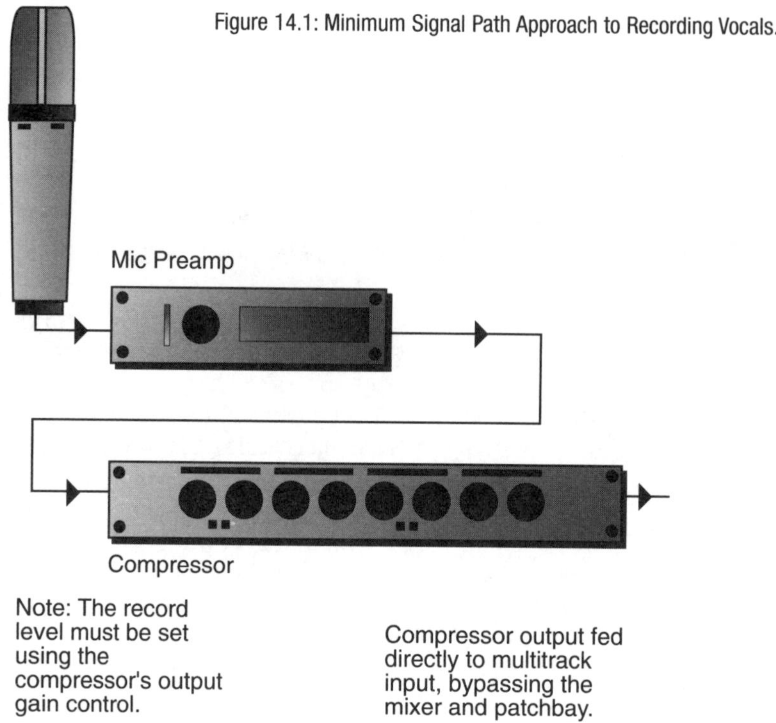

Mic Preamp
Compressor
Note: The record level must be set using the compressor's output gain control.
Compressor output fed directly to multitrack input, bypassing the mixer and patchbay.

Figure 14.1: Minimum Signal Path Approach to Recording Vocals.

machine and may also offer some form of level control, allowing the recording level to be optimised. Line level signals include the outputs from guitar preamps and speaker simulators, as well as active guitars, basses and some electronic instruments. Passive guitars have high impedance pickups which, in theory, means that an active DI box will give the best matching. Even so, a good passive (transformer) DI box can give surprisingly good results and may produce a more natural sound than an active model. The lower input impedance may also reduce the effect of interference on the signal, giving a cleaner result.

Guitar speaker simulators and preamps designed specifically for direct recording are very effective these days; whereas a few years ago nobody would have dreamt of using anything other than a mic to record a guitar, the direct approach is currently very popular, even on serious guitar album projects. The advantages of this way of working are immediately obvious — the sound the performer hears over the monitors is the same sound that is going to tape, and perhaps more importantly, there is complete isolation between the guitar and any other instrument being recorded at the same time. Acoustic spill problems are completely eliminated, making the guitar as easy to record as the electronic keyboard synthesizer.

Rhythm Guitar

Clean rhythm sounds can be recorded directly to tape using a simple DI box, though some EQ is usually necessary to simulate the way in which guitar amplifiers are voiced.

★TECHNIQUE

◆ A significant amount of upper mid boost is generally needed, and if this may be achieved using something like an upper-mid sweep equaliser tuned to between 3 and 6kHz, the necessary brightness can be produced with less of a noise penalty than would be the case if the high shelving EQ were used.

◆ It can be advantageous to over-boost the upper mid and then back off the high frequency shelving control a little to compensate. This will result in a reduction in high frequency noise without unduly dulling the guitar sound.

◆ A popular approach to recording rhythm guitar is to feed the guitar, via a DI box, into a suitable compressor, and then directly to tape. A suitable compressor is really any model that sounds good, though valve compressors are often chosen for their warm, smooth sound. In general, if a compressor sounds good on vocals, it will work well with guitars.

Overdriven Guitar

Recording overdriven guitar is less straightforward, and if an overdrive pedal is patched directly into a tape recorder, the result will be quite unlike that produced by miking an amplifier. The reason for this was touched upon in my chapter on recording guitars, and is mainly to do with the way in which a guitar speaker and its enclosure modify the electric guitar's sound. Guitar speakers generally use a large driver with no separate mid-range units or tweeters, which gives them a severely restricted frequency response. Indeed, if full-range speakers were used, the overdrive sound would be most raspy and unpleasant. The cabinet design also affects the way in which the speaker behaves, and an analysis of the speaker and cabinet combination reveals a complex low-pass filter response. If this is emulated using electronic filters, it is possible to take the output from an overdriven guitar preamp or pedal, process it via the filter and record it directly.

The result is surprisingly close to the sound produced by a close-miked amplifier but it isn't exactly the same. That's because most 'speaker simulator' units fail to duplicate the complex distortions that occur when a loudspeaker is overdriven and they also fail to take into account the characteristics or positioning of the microphone normally used to record the guitar amp. Even so, a little extra work with EQ and a little added artificial reverb or ambience at the mixing stage can render the differences very small indeed. Indeed, over the past decade, the popular rock guitar sound has changed significantly, making it more difficult to judge the authenticity of any electronic simulation. Speaker simulator circuitry is becoming more common in guitar preamps and guitar multi-effects units, though the results that can be achieved vary drastically from model to model.

Speaker Simulator

The other popular form of speaker simulator is, in effect, a combined filter and power soak which is used to replace the speaker in a conventional guitar amplifier. Supplied as add-on boxes, these are available in both active and passive versions and produce either a line level or mic level output from amplifiers rated up to 100 watts or so. Some have virtually no controls, while others may have voicing switches and equalisation enabling them to simulate many different types of guitar speaker system. Used with a good valve amplifier, these produce what many feel is a more authentic, basic tone than solid-state preamps and effects units, though any effects must be added separately.

The line output type of speaker simulator may be connected directly to a tape machine, but the type with a mic level output needs to be recorded via a separate mic preamp or via the mic input of the mixing console. It can be argued that an overdriven guitar sound is so noisy and distorted that there is little to be gained in bypassing the mixer completely, but ultimately, the decision must be taken by the individual engineer. It is certainly worth making a test recording, both direct and via the desk, to see how significant the difference really is. You may be very surprised. It is common practice to use a compressor after the speaker simulator. Figure 14.2 shows how a speaker simulator is connected.

Active Guitars

Active guitars and basses may be plugged directly into the mixing console without any impedance matching problems, but some form of speaker simulation is still necessary when working with overdriven guitar sounds, and basses generally need to be compressed. In my own experience, active guitars tend to be noisier than guitars with passive pickups.

Keyboards

Keyboard instruments, samplers, drum machines and synth modules can be recorded directly, but most have relatively low output levels, ranging from -20 to -10dBv. This means that it may be possible to plug them directly into

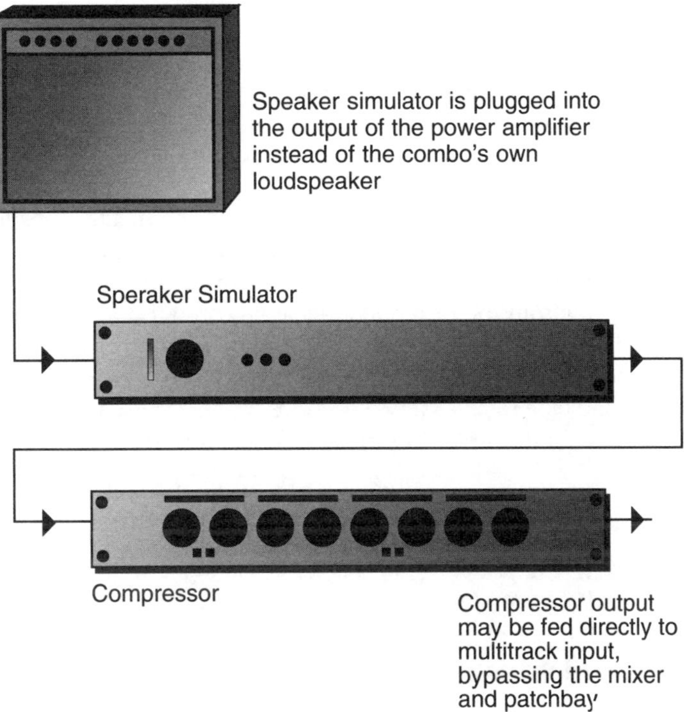
Speaker simulator is plugged into the output of the power amplifier instead of the combo's own loudspeaker
Speraker Simulator
Compressor
Compressor output may be fed directly to multitrack input, bypassing the mixer and patchbay
Note: Though the use of a compressor is not mandatory, its inclusion generally produces a more appealing sound by creating a more even tone and enhancing the natural sustain of the guitar

Figure 14.2: Using a Speaker Simulator

a semi-pro machine operating at -10dBv, but the vast majority will have insufficient output to produce a healthy recording level when used with professional tape machines. Furthermore, some instruments have no proper output level controls, especially drum machines with multiple outputs.

Again, the answer is to use an active DI box, which will improve the impedance matching and provide the additional gain needed. As with the electric guitar, it is up to the individual to decide whether it is worth going to the trouble of recording direct or whether recording via the mixer is adequate. The majority of synthesizers still have a disappointing audio specification and it is arguable whether the trip through a mixing console would make the situation significantly worse. As more recordings are now being made with all the MIDI sound sources played live into the mix from a suitably synchronised sequencer, this question may never arise.

The only keyboard system that must be miked rather than DI'd is the Leslie cabinet where it is common to use separate mics on the horns and the bass rotor. If possible use a stereo mic arrangement on the rotary horns.

Mixer Noise

Even if recordings are made through the mixing console, there are ways to ensure that the signal remains as clean as possible. For example, if a mixer has direct channel outputs or even insert points, a signal could be taken directly from the mixer channel and routed to the tape recorder; this would bypass the routing switches, the pan control and the group output electronics. Of course, this is only viable when one channel is being recorded to one tape track — if two or more channels have to be mixed together, then there is little choice but to use the desk's normal routing system.

Having said this, there are steps that can be taken to minimise the amount of noise added to the signal on its way to tape. Most consoles have an EQ bypass button, and if no EQ is being added at the recording stage, switching the EQ out of circuit will shorten the signal path slightly.

Muting And Routing

Most people instinctively mute any mixer channels that are not being routed and nearly all will set the faders at zero, but this, perhaps surprisingly, doesn't entirely prevent the channel from contributing noise to the mix.

★TIP

When recording, make sure that any unused channels are not only muted but also that they are not routed to any of the group outputs — in other words, ensure that all their routing buttons are up. Even if unused channels are muted and all the gain controls turned down, they will contribute noise to any mix buss to which they are routed simply by virtue of being connected to the buss via their routing switches.

This is more important when you come to mix, as any unused channel with its Left/Right routing button down will be contributing unnecessary noise to the final mix. To prove this to yourself, route all your mixer channels to the main stereo output and turn all the channel faders right down. If you have channel mute buttons, set these to their mute positions. Now, turn up the monitor level control until you can hear the console hiss through the monitors. Without changing anything else, go along the console switching the Left/Right routing buttons to their up positions and I guarantee you'll be surprised by the drop in hiss. The more channels you have on your desk, the greater will be the benefit of careful routing.

Monitor Section

The other danger area is the monitor section of the desk which, on some models, is routed directly to the Left/Right buss with no means of disconnecting it. On some consoles, the monitor mutes actually disconnect the monitor channels from the mix buss but on others, especially budget desks with MIDI muting, they mute the signal but still leave the monitor routed. There's not much you can do about this, other than be aware of the problem. Repeating the previous noise test using the monitor mute buttons will tell you whether they are simply mutes or whether they do switch the monitors off the mix buss — if the noise goes down as you mute the monitors, you're in luck — the mute switches are really routing buttons.

The same rules apply to auxiliary sends, and many an innocent effects unit has been blamed for being noisy when in fact the mixer has been to blame. Few mixing desks offer the facility to switch individual aux sends off their respective aux busses when they are not being used, but there are several mixers that allow their aux sends to be routed to a choice of aux send busses.This is particularly common in the mid-price market, where a console may have eight aux busses but only four aux send controls which can be switched between them.

★TIP

Unless all the aux send busses are in use, one useful trick is to route any unused sends to unused effects busses. For example, if you can route aux 1 and 2 as a pair to either aux busses 1,2 or 3,4 you could designate aux busses 3,4 as being unused and route any unused sends there. This obviously restricts the number of available aux sends, but there are many occasions when a specific effect is required on only one mixer channel, in which case the effects unit can be fed from the direct channel output or insert send point. There's no reason why an effect shouldn't be patched in via the channel insert point, but as most modern effects have stereo outputs, some other method must generally be sought if the effect is to be kept in stereo.

Direct Outputs

Using the channel's direct output as an effects send has the advantage that the send level will be controlled by the channel fader, but unless significant gain changes are planned during the mix, it is possible to get away with using the insert send. Indeed, if the effects returns can be arranged to come up on an adjacent channel, it should be possible to move the faders together, which gets around the problem of using the insert send point. Figure 14.3 shows how this is set up.

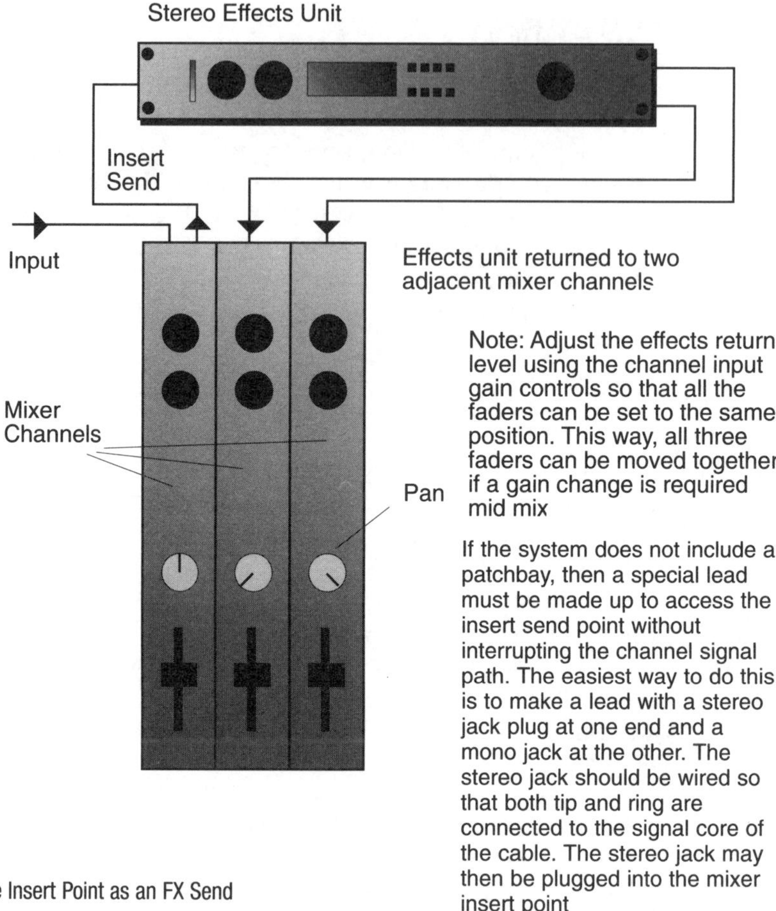

Stereo Effects Unit
Insert
Send
Input
Effects unit returned to two
adjacent mixer channels
Note: Adjust the effects return
level using the channel input
gain controls so that all the
faders can be set to the same
position. This way, all three
faders can be moved together
if a gain change is required
mid mix
Mixer
Channels
Pan
If the system does not include a
patchbay, then a special lead
must be made up to access the
insert send point without
interrupting the channel signal
path. The easiest way to do this
is to make a lead with a stereo
jack plug at one end and a
mono jack at the other. The
stereo jack should be wired so
that both tip and ring are
connected to the signal core of
the cable. The stereo jack may
then be plugged into the mixer
insert point

Figure 14.3: Using the Insert Point as an FX Send

A more elegant solution is to use the insert send or direct output from the channel carrying the signal to feed the mono input of the effects unit, exactly as before, but this time the channel is not routed to the mix. Its only purpose is to provide an input feed to the effects unit.

◆ The two effect outputs are connected to the inputs of two spare channels.

◆ The effect/dry balance can then be set using the mix control on the effects unit, and the two channels can be panned left and right to create a stereo effect.

◆ With most effects units, using the mono input will position the dry portion of the sound in the centre of the mix with the stereo effects outputs left and right.

This variation is shown in Figure 14.4, the only restriction being that the dry portion of the sound will always be panned to the centre of the mix.

Gain Structure

Finally, all this effort will go to waste if the gain structure of the mixer isn't set up properly.

◆ The channel input trims should be set up using the meters in conjunction with the PFL or Solo buttons.

◆ The mix should be arranged so that the average fader position is around the three-quarters full position.

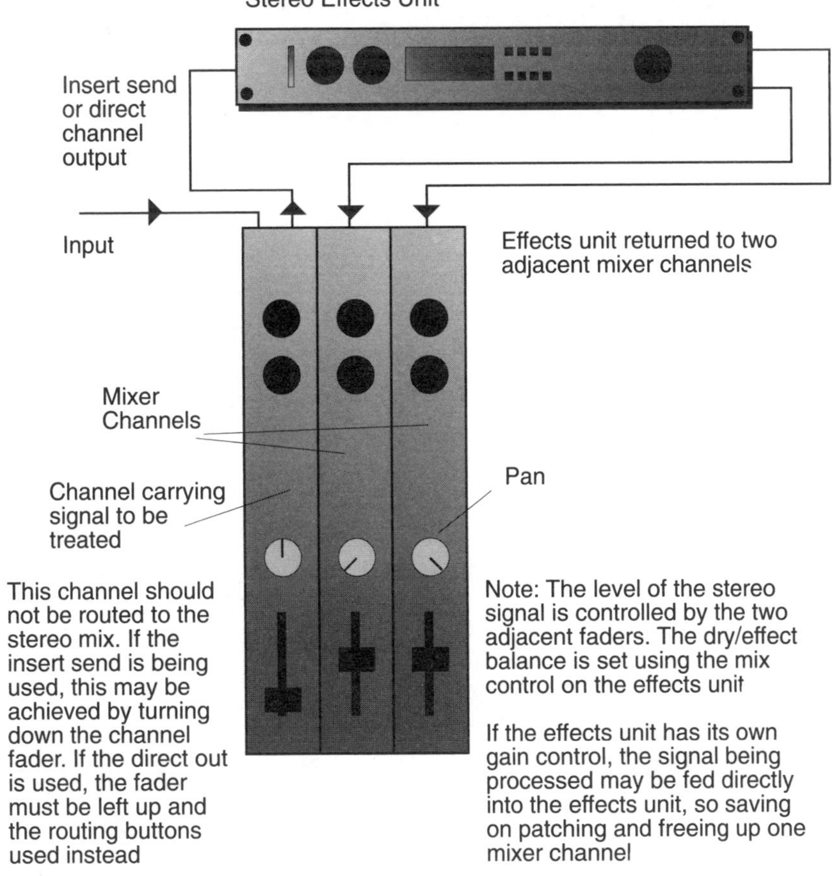
Stereo Effects Unit
Insert send or direct channel output
Input
Effects unit returned to two adjacent mixer channels
Mixer Channels
Channel carrying signal to be treated
Pan
This channel should not be routed to the stereo mix. If the insert send is being used, this may be achieved by turning down the channel fader. If the direct out is used, the fader must be left up and the routing buttons used instead
Note: The level of the stereo signal is controlled by the two adjacent faders. The dry/effect balance is set using the mix control on the effects unit
If the effects unit has its own gain control, the signal being processed may be fed directly into the effects unit, so saving on patching and freeing up one mixer channel

Figure 14.4: Alternative Effects Patch

◆ Set the aux send controls so that the highest one is almost full up and use the aux send master or the input gain on the effects unit to get the right signal going into the effects processor.

◆ Don't forget to optimise the level trim on any channels being used to carry effects returns, and turn any unused sends right down.

◆ Always be suspicious if you have output level controls (or effects unit input controls) set at minimum. If you use one control to knock the signal level down and the next one in line to build it up again, you're setting up the ideal conditions for unwanted noise. Try to arrange everything so that all gain controls are set in 'sensible' positions.

The measures outlined above may appear unnecessarily complicated, but the few extra moments taken to set up the console properly will yield a significant difference in signal quality. Eliminating noise at source is infinitely more satisfactory than trying to remove it with gates or dynamic filters at a later stage.

chapter 15

mixing

Watching a really skilled engineer at work can be an intimidating experience — the real experts can move along the desk pushing up the faders one at a time, having an almost perfectly balanced mix by the time they reach the end. Somehow they have an instinct for balance, and what they achieve seemingly by magic, we have to arrive at by hard work.

It helps before starting the mix to organise logical groups of sounds into subgroups, which means that the mix can be handled with fewer faders. Most recordings have the drums spread over several tape tracks, and life is far easier if these are routed to a pair of adjacent group faders to form a stereo subgroup. Similarly, backing vocals can be assigned to subgroups along with any other sections that seem logical.

Balance

If the basic tracks have been recorded properly, it should be possible to set up a reasonable initial balance without resorting to EQ. Effects need not be added right from the outset, but it helps to have the necessary effects units patched in and ready for use, and some vocal reverb helps paint the picture. Switch the EQ to bypass on all channels where it isn't being used and ensure that any unused mixer channels are not only muted but also unrouted — in other words, all the routing buttons should be in their 'up' position. This will prevent the channel from contributing to the mix buss noise of the console, and will help achieve a quieter final mix. All unused aux sends should be set at zero level, and the loudest sends should be between three quarters and full up. Again, this helps to reduce noise. All console inputs should be trimmed using the PFL metering system if your console allows trim on mixdown. Likewise, all the effects units should be checked for correct input levels. If it is possible to route unused sends to an aux buss that isn't being used, this can reduce mix noise considerably, while any effect intended to process a single channel will produce the best audio quality if connected via the channel insert point.

Having attended to these basic niceties, my own way of working is to sort out the drum and bass balance first, but this should not be refined too much, as the apparent balance will change once the rest of the instruments and voices are in the mix. Once the rhythm section is sounding good, the remaining faders can be brought up one at a time until a reasonable overall balance has been achieved. It's only when all the instruments are in place that you should start to worry about the finer points of EQ and balance, because things sound so different when they are heard in isolation.

Of course, some engineers and producers insist that the only possible way to work is to put all the faders up to start with and then adjust for a balance. Don't be put off by this, though, because I've spoken to many well-regarded engineers and producers who admit that they don't have this natural gift for balance — they have to work just as hard as the rest of us!

Stereo Positions

Once a reasonable balance has been achieved, you can start to work on the effects being used and the stereo positioning of the different sounds. Bass drums, bass guitars and bass synths are invariably panned to the centre to anchor the mix and to spread the load of these high energy frequencies over both speakers. Similarly, lead vocals are usually positioned centre stage because that's where we expect the vocalist to be.

The position of backing vocals is less rigid, and can be split so that some are left and some are right; they can be left in the centre, or they can all be grouped in one position off-centre. I like to hear different backing vocal lines coming in from different sides, but this decision is purely artistic — there is no absolute right and wrong. If recorded vocals exhibit any sibilance problems, a de-esser should be patched in before proceeding.

Once the mix is almost there, it can be very helpful to listen to the balance from an adjacent room with the adjoining door left open. Although I can find no logical explanation for the phenomenon, any slight balance problems really show up when a mix is auditioned in this way, and most engineers and producers who've discovered this way of checking a mix use it regularly. Figure 15.1 shows a typical panning arrangement for a pop song.

Level Correction

A good mix will almost 'fly' itself, but some parts invariably need level corrections throughout the mix. Obvious examples are instrumental solos and changes in effects levels, but even on vocals with heavy compression, it may still be necessary to adjust the odd vocal phrase by a dB or so to make it sit properly. If the mix is being conducted manually, responsibility for the various fader adjustments can be devolved amongst the various band

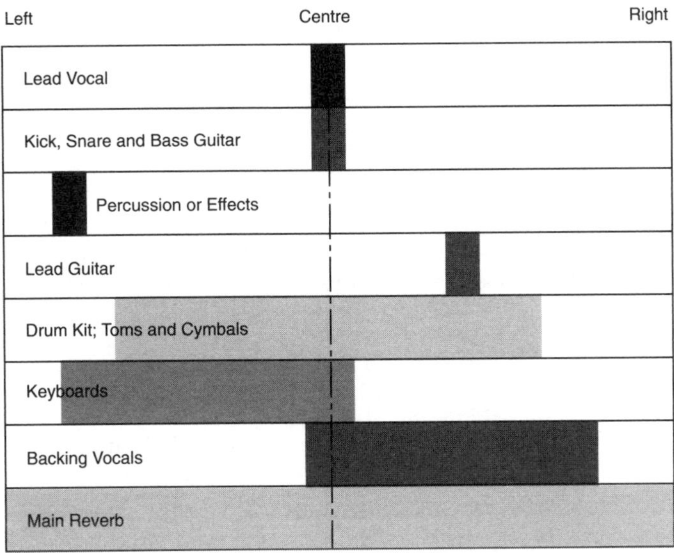

Figure 15.1: Typical Stereo Panning Scenario

members. The level settings should be clearly marked with wax pencil and each person should have a note of the various tape counter positions at which levels have to be changed. Of course, if an automated mixing system is available, these changes can be handled quite automatically.

If a track requires a fade-out ending, this may be performed manually or with an autofader. Fades are seldom shorter than 15 seconds and may be as long as 30, so it is important to ensure that there is enough recorded material to cover the duration of the fade. If you know in advance that the album is going to be compiled using a hard disk editing system, it might be wiser to leave the fades until the final editing stage, where they can be controlled more precisely and will fade into true silence.

I've already covered some of the console settings that affect noise, but we also have to consider noise that is part of the recorded sound. We have breath noise from singers, hum and hiss from guitars and digital background noise from synths, samplers and drum machines. If sequenced MIDI instruments are being used, it is often possible to program level changes via MIDI, but we have to be careful, as some instruments put out a more or less constant level of unwanted noise, regardless of the level of the voice currently playing. We should always strive to use these machines as close to their maximum volume setting as is practical, as this will usually give the best signal-to-noise ratio. Likewise, it is possible to mute instruments via the sequencer, but this just stops the sequenced parts from playing and doesn't affect the background noise in any way.

Gates And Mutes

Gates or expanders are very effective in cleaning up electronic instruments, though care must be taken to match the release time of the gate to the sound being processed. In some cases, it may be possible to use a pair of gates over a stereo subgroup; this offers the advantage that fewer gates are needed. It must be remembered, though, that gates can only keep the noise down during pauses and can do nothing when a signal is present.

Perhaps the most dramatic effect of MIDI muting or gating can be noticed right at the beginning of the song where perfect silence reigns until the first note is played. It shouldn't be necessary to mute every short silence, but it is a good idea to mute the vocal track during instrumental solos or bridge sections, and to mute the lead guitar track both before and after the solo.

MIDI console muting can be very useful for dealing with source noise, and though it may take a little time to set up, the results are usually well worth the trouble. It is necessary to go through each tape track and set up the mute points individually, but once they're right, they'll be right every time you run the mix. If you can arrange muting and unmuting on a beat, it may help to disguise any discontinuity or change in noise level.

The mutes on most MIDI desks are very quiet in operation, but I know that on some models there is an audible click if many mutes are switched at the same time. If this is the case, it should be possible to work around the problem by using the mutes on the subgroups or master output faders rather than attempting to switch all the channels at once.

Noise Filters

In the event that some of your sound sources are noticeably noisy even when being played, it might be desirable to use a single-ended noise reduction unit to minimise the noise. These are dynamic filter units which filter out higher frequencies as sounds decay; used carefully, they can bring about a dramatic decrease in noise without affecting the sound of the wanted signal. However, they do tend to affect the tail end of long reverbs so it is probably prudent to assign all the noisy sounds to a stereo subgroup and process just this. This leaves the higher quality sounds and effects returns unprocessed, which will give a more natural result.

Mix Processing

Producers tend to be divided when it comes to applying further processing to the overall stereo mix. The more puritanical might say that there is no need to process the mix once you've got it right, while others will insist on putting it through their favourite compressor, equaliser or exciter. There can be no definitive right or wrong answer to this question; in pop music production, the end always justifies the means (so long as it is within budget!). However, we can explore some of the implications inherent in post-mix processing.

Overall Compression

Compressing a complete mix reduces the difference between the quietest parts of the mix and the loudest. If the highest levels peak at around the same value as they did before compression, then it follows that average level must be higher, and this is reflected in a subjective increase in musical energy. However, a sound will only appear to be loud if it has a quieter sound to contrast with, so there is a danger of making a piece of music sound quieter by compressing it too much.

When compressing a mix, the attack time of the compressor is usually extended slightly to allow transient sounds such as drums to punch through with more power, though the best setting can only be determined by ear, as every piece of music is different. It is also true that some compressors perform disappointingly when used on complete mixes, whereas others produce results that appear to be little short of magic. As a very general rule, soft-knee compressors produce the most subtle results — but do you always want to be subtle? Sadly, the compressors that work best in this application also seem to cost the most!

Overall EQ

Equalising the whole mix might seem a little reckless, but some equalisers seem to improve the sound noticeably, even when very subtle settings are used. Music can be made to appear louder by cutting the mid-range slightly, as this emulates the response curve of the human ear. It may also be necessary to equalise a mix if it has been made in a studio with an inaccurate monitor system. Indeed, there are so many inaccurate control rooms around that when a master tape is sent to the cutting room to be prepared for record or CD mastering, it is very common for the engineer to apply a degree of corrective EQ at that stage.

Cutting rooms don't always have the nicest sounding equalisers, so if the producer has access to a good monitoring system (and many take their own with them), it may be preferable to make any changes at this stage, where they can be controlled and evaluated on an artistic rather than a purely technical basis.

Exciters

It is not uncommon to treat a whole mix with an exciter or a dynamic equaliser. These tend to emphasise certain parts of the frequency spectrum in a way that is related to the dynamics of the signal, so that transient sounds are given more definition. This increases the perceived sense of loudness, which helps a record stand out from the competition on the radio or on the dance floor. The exciter actually synthesises harmonics based on the existing programme material and so may be more suitable for dealing with a mix that is insufficiently bright. The dynamic equaliser creates no new harmonics but, in effect, redistributes what is already there and so may give a smoother sound. Dynamic equalisers can also be used to add power at the bass end, whereas most exciters simply work at the very high frequency end of the audio spectrum. Newer models, however, increasingly address the bottom end of the frequency spectrum by offering some type of bass enhancement.

Monitoring Alternatives

Before a final mix is approved, it should be checked on different speaker systems, including car systems and domestic hi-fi. Large studio monitoring systems can be very misleading and it is essential to test the mix at a moderate listening level on a small pair of speakers. Avoid the temptation to mix at too high a volume, as this will only serve to adversely affect your hearing judgement.Ultimately, the best test is to listen to your mix at the same level as you would expect the end user to listen at.

The Master

DAT has become a standard mastering medium, even though it is still, strictly speaking, only a semi-pro or domestic format. If there is a choice, make the master at a sampling frequency of 44.1 kHz, as this will save the need to have the sample rate converted when making a CD master. With any form of digital recording, you must keep a very close eye on recording levels, because there is no leeway above 0VU — the sound immediately clips and distortion is usually audible. Try to arrange your levels so that the peaks reach between -3 and -6VU on the DAT machine's meters; this should provide an adequate margin of safety while still giving a good signal-to-noise performance.

Once the master tape has been recorded, it must be backed up, particularly if it is on DAT as, contrary to some expectations, DAT isn't 100% reliable. To back up a DAT to another DAT, make a clone by connecting the machines via their digital audio links. It is safest to leave at least ten seconds of unrecorded tape at the beginning of a DAT cassette — if trouble is going to occur, it usually occurs here — and the backup should be clearly marked and stored in a safe place.

It is also worth backing up DAT masters to open reel tape. Interestingly, in many cases, the analogue copy sounds subjectively better than the DAT! This is undoubtedly due to the many small imperfections of analogue recording that contribute to its alleged warm, comfortable sound.

Labelling

All session tapes should be clearly labelled, as should any unused mixes and out-takes you wish to keep. Include information such as:

- The track format
- The tape speed
- The noise reduction system used
- Track titles
- Track start times and end times
- Track durations

Also ask the engineer to put a set of calibration tones at the start of any analogue masters or backups. Though calibration tones shouldn't be necessary with DAT, tape duplicators and mastering houses like to have a 1kHz tone recorded at the start of a tape, usually around 20 seconds in duration, at a level of -10VU. The actual level is less important than writing on the box what the level is!

If the master tape is intended for album production, the individual tracks must spaced apart by the required duration of silence. With analogue tape, this is achieved by splicing lengths of plastic leader tape or blank recording tape between the individual songs, the actual length depending very much on how the previous song ends and on how the next one starts. For example, the space required after a song with a fade-out ending might need to be only a couple of seconds; on the other hand, if one songs ends with a bang and the next starts equally as abruptly, anything up to five seconds might be needed. There are no hard and fast rules about this, but you can instinctively feel if a gap is more than half a second too short or too long.

Track Spacing

Spacing songs on a DAT tape is far less easy than doing the same job with analogue tape, because DATs can't stop and start in the same instant way as analogue machines. Using two DAT machines, it is possible to make a reasonable job of compiling an album simply by using the pause button on the second machine to start and stop it, but it is difficult to time gaps to an accuracy of better than one second. It is far better to use a hard disk editing system, where the gaps can be timed to millisecond accuracy and where unwanted noise before and after songs can be cut out with surgical precision. With such systems, it is usually possible to handle precision fade-outs and fade-ins, level changes and occasionally, digital equalisation. Some also offer digital time or pitch compression, but in my experience, this is seldom satisfactory.

Stereo Width Tricks

When it comes to stereo, most of what we do in the recording studio is out-and-out fraud! In real life, our hearing systems establish the direction of a sound source by evaluating a multitude of parameters including phase, amplitude and spectral content; in the studio we cheat and use pan pots. True, there are proper stereo miking techniques that capture many of the nuances of a real-life soundfield, but when it comes to producing pop music, we are inclined to rely on pan pots to change the balance between the left and right speakers, effects with synthesised stereo outputs, and electronic musical instruments whose stereo outputs are artificially created by routing different mixes of signal to the left and right outputs.

Even so, there are some simple but effective processing techniques that can be used to create the illusion of stereo, even when the signal being treated is mono. In multitrack recording, such processing is very useful, especially when working with 4- or 8-track where parts often have to be bounced into mono to conserve track space.

All In The Mind

Sophisticated though the human hearing system is, it would appear that it is far easier to fool than, for example, our vision. Digital reverberators create the illusion of stereo simply by using different sets of delay taps on the left and right channels, giving rise to two sets of reverberation patterns, which, although similar in their overall parameters, differ in their fine detail in essentially random ways. It seems that our hearing systems are so keen to make sense of the world around us that they eagerly accept this random information and use it to construct an imaginary, auditory world in which the processed sound exists.

This provides us with one very simple way to turn a mono sound into something that sounds like stereo — add reverb to it. The trouble is that we might want the sound to appear to be in stereo, but we don't want to add any noticeable amount of reverb. In that case, choose a reverb setting that provides an early reflections pattern but without the following reverb. Such settings add a relatively small number of closely-spaced reflections to the sound with different patterns in the left and right channels. The result is that the sound takes on a sense of space but with no apparent reverberation.

★TIP

A similar effect can be achieved using a less sophisticated reverb unit by selecting a very short, bright reverb setting (around half a second decay or even less) and then increasing the mix of reverb until the sound takes on the required extra dimension. If the reverb time is set short enough, the effect is not dissimilar from that created by an early reflections pattern setting, though with some of the cheaper reverb units, short settings might tend to sound a touch 'ringy', especially if percussive sounds are involved.

Delay

There are lots of tricks you can try with a simple delay unit that have the effect of widening the stereo image, but you must be aware that most of these are not completely mono compatible, so keep pressing the mono button on your mixer or power amplifier to see if what you've done has unacceptable side-effects when listening in mono. This is particularly important for broadcast material, as there are still many people listening to mono radios and mono TV sets, but insisting on absolute mono compatibility does place severe restrictions on what you can do — after all, real life isn't actually mono compatible when you come to think about it!

Here's the simplest trick:

★TECHNIQUE

• Pan your mono signal to one side of the stereo field and pan a delayed version of the same sound, at the same level, to the other side. The delay should be very short so as not to produce an obvious echo — between 2mS and 20mS will work.

You'll notice something very interesting when you try this — even though the level of signal in both speakers is equal, the sound will appear to be coming from the speaker that's receiving the undelayed sound. At the same time, it will sound wider than a straight mono source. The reason for this is tied up with the way in which our brains process sound; if a sound comes from our left, it will reach the left ear before it reaches the right ear, and this small time difference is one way the brain works out direction. In recording, this is known as the precedence effect. Figure 15.2 shows a simple way to set up this process using a basic DDL and a mixer with channel insert points. The DDL should be set to between 2mS and 20mS delay time with no modulation and no feedback. The mix control should be set to give only the delayed sound and none of the direct sound. On a manual unit, this usually means the fully clockwise setting of the mix control.

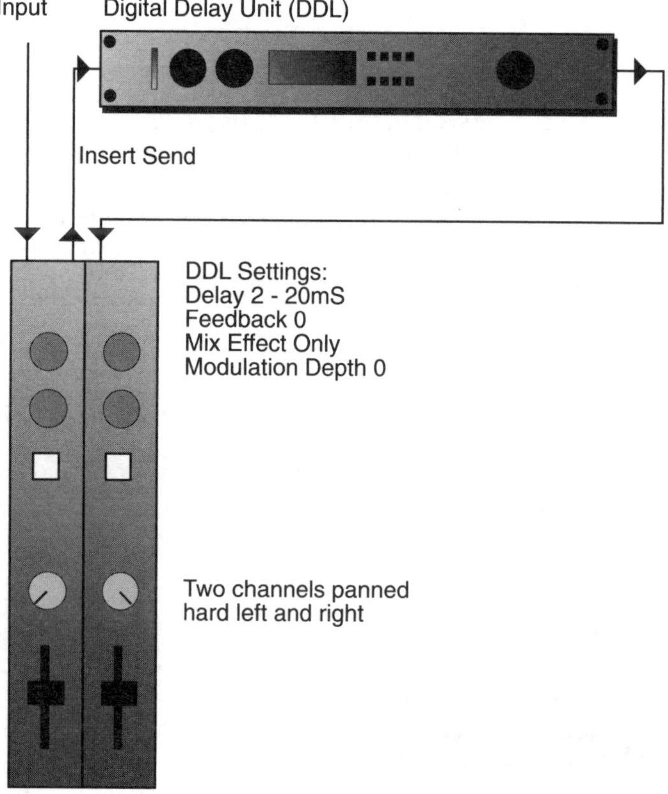

Figure 15.2: Delay Panning

Another effect which can be produced using the same setup is stereo chorus. This is something I discovered back in my serious gigging days at a time when stereo chorus units didn't exist. I used to have two guitar amps, one fed from the straight guitar sound and the other fed through a mono chorus pedal. Straight away I noticed this combination created the illusion of movement between the speakers, and from the normal listening position, it wasn't easy to tell which speaker was producing the straight sound and which one had been put though a chorus. When I got into home recording, I took this technique into the studio and found it incredibly useful for creating really wide, dynamic chorus effects for guitar and synthesizer. Even though stereo chorus units then started to become available, I don't think any of them ever sounded wider than my simple set-up. Furthermore, if you have a mixer that has plenty of line input gain, you can set up this effect using a standard pedal chorus unit rather than tying up your multi-effects unit for the job. And, by feeding the effect from a post-fade aux send, you can add different amounts of chorus to different instruments in a mix. The only limitation here is that to get the full effect of the stereo spread, all the sounds being processed should be panned more or less to one side of the mix and the output from the chorus unit to the other. To achieve a suitable chorus setting:

★TECHNIQUE

◆ The DDL should be set with a delay time between 10 and 50mS with a modulation rate of between 1Hz and 5Hz.

◆ The modulation depth is then brought up slowly until the required chorus effect is created.

◆ The mix control should be set at 50% delayed sound, 50% direct sound — which is generally the centre position on a manual unit.

True chorus uses no feedback, but some feedback may be added to create an effect somewhere between chorus and flanging if preferred. As a rule, when setting up modulated delay effects, the longer the delay time, the less modulation depth is required.

An interesting variation on this effect is:

★TECHNIQUE

◆ Pan the dry sound to the centre.

◆ Pan the chorused sound to one side

◆ Pan the same chorused sound processed via a channel with the phase button depressed to the other side.

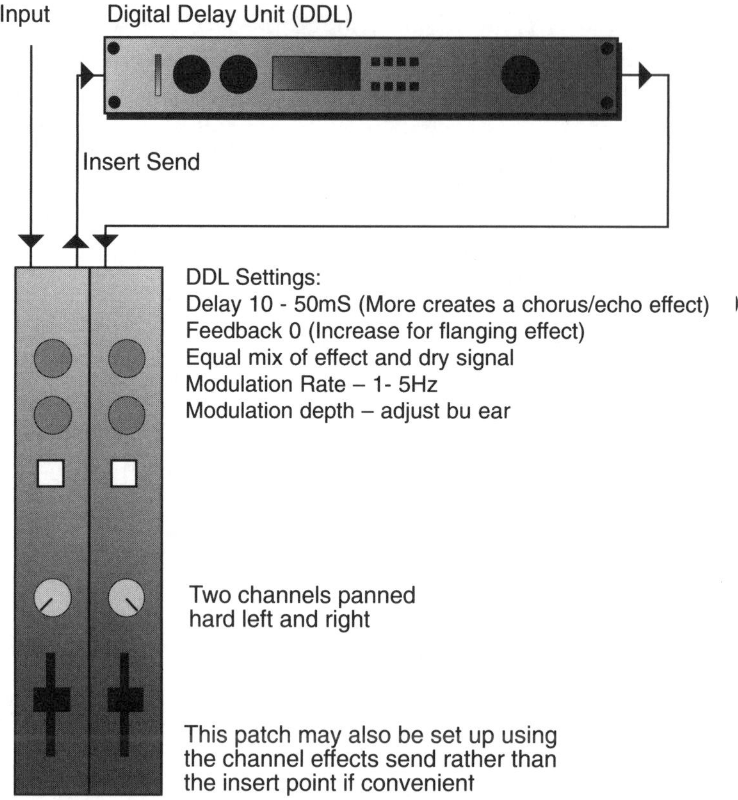

Input
Digital Delay Unit (DDL)
Insert Send
DDL Settings:
Delay 10 - 50mS (More creates a chorus/echo effect)
Feedback 0 (Increase for flanging effect)
Equal mix of effect and dry signal
Modulation Rate – 1- 5Hz
Modulation depth – adjust bu ear
Two channels panned
hard left and right
This patch may also be set up using
the channel effects send rather than
the insert point if convenient

Figure 15.3: Pseudo Stereo Chorus

This also gives a wide stereo spread, but if the sound is subsequently summed to mono, though the original sound survives intact, all the chorus effect is cancelled out. This is obviously undesirable for serious recording which might be used for radio or TV airplay.

Using Equalisers

One effective but decidedly artificial method for making mono appear to be in stereo was devised back in the early days of stereo recording, when old mono records were frequently reprocessed to sound wider in stereo. This particular technique used a stereo graphic equaliser set-up, the input signal being split to feed both channels of the equaliser. The idea was to set the two equalisers differently so they'd emphasise different parts of the mix, which could then be panned left and right. The method outlined in Figure 15.4 is a refinement of this idea and has the additional benefit that it can be accomplished with a single-channel equaliser. In general, the more bands

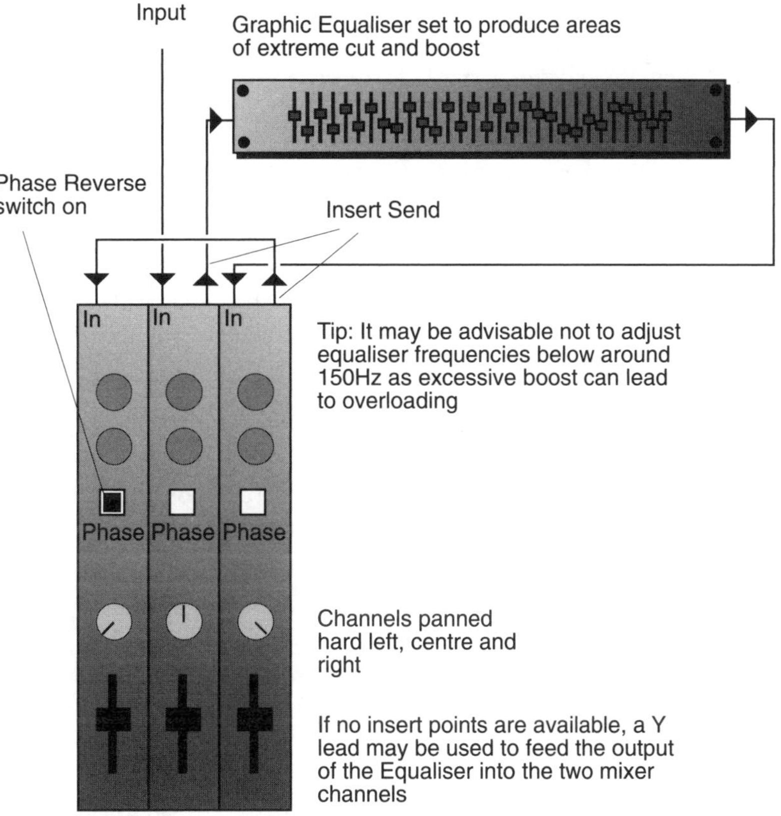

Figure 15.4: Pseudo Stereo Using EQ

the better, but you can get a useful result from just about any graphic equaliser. The patch may be set up either using a Y lead to split the output from the graphic equaliser or by using the channel insert sends as shown.

Here's how:

★TECHNIQUE

◆ Feed the original signal directly to a mixer channel and pan it dead centre.

◆ Take a feed from that channel's insert send and feed it into the graphic equaliser.

◆ Split the output of the equaliser into two using a Y-lead, and feed into two more mixer channels, one panned hard left and the other right; the phase invert button is depressed on one of these two channels — it doesn't matter which one.

◆ To create the stereo effect, the equaliser needs to be set to produce a number of bumps and dips in the audio spectrum, and though just about any setting will produce a useful result (for example, setting the faders alternately up and down), it is more productive to try to identify specific areas of the spectrum where certain things are going on — guitars, keyboard pads and so on, and then home in on these.

How does it work? Assuming that the channel panned to the right is the one with the phase button down, the left signal will be a sum of the direct signal (centre) and the equalised signal (left). The right hand signal, on the other hand, will be the difference between the direct signal and the equalised signal because of the action of the phase invert button. This means that what constitutes an EQ peak in the left channel will manifest itself as an equal and opposite dip in the right channel and vice versa. The neat thing about working in this way is that if the signal is heard in mono, the contribution of the equaliser cancels itself out and so you're left with just the original mono signal. However, don't assume that the process is 100% mono compatible because the subjective level appears to drop when the left and right components are cancelled out. How serious this is depends on how much of the equalised sound is added to the direct sound.

It is important to get the level of the two channels fed from the equaliser as similar as possible. The easiest way to do this is to mute the direct signal using the channel mute and listen to just the two channels fed from the equaliser. If these are, temporarily, panned to the centre, the signal will cancel completely when both are exactly equal in level. Once this has been verified, they can be panned back to their respective sides and the direct signal turned back on.

The result of this processing trick is quite interesting, in that the stereo image does take on an extra dimension, but you can't actually pick out where the sounds are supposed to be coming from. It's rather like reverberation in that respect — the illusion of space is created, but no real directional information is provided. Though it's no substitute for true stereo recording, this trick and others like it make it possible to produce a wide and interesting stereo image when working on 4-track, where several musical parts have to be bounced into mono.

Feel The Width

Here's a simple but nevertheless effective technique for making the stereo spread appear to be wider than the spacing of the stereo loudspeakers.

★ TIP

This particular trick has been used in ghetto blasters for many years and simply involves taking some of the right hand signal and feeding it, out of phase, to the left hand channel, and vice versa. The phase effects introduced in this way appear to push the sound out beyond the boundaries of the speakers, but if too much of the out-of-phase signal is added, the stereo positioning actually appears to swap sides. For this reason, it is vital to make sure that the unprocessed stereo signal remains the loudest part of the mix. Too much out-of-phase component also makes the mix sound 'phasey', and though different people perceive this in different ways, I find it physically uncomfortable; try it yourself by setting an equal mix of direct and out-of-phase sound and standing exactly between the speakers.

Ideally, you need to mix the out-of-phase sounds low enough to avoid this effect. Though it's no substitute for Roland's RSS 3D sound system or Q-Sound processing, this simple trick can be usefully applied to individual subgroups within a mix or to stereo effects returns to add an extra dimension to a mix. And, because the added components are equal and opposite, they cancel completely when the signal is summed to mono, so

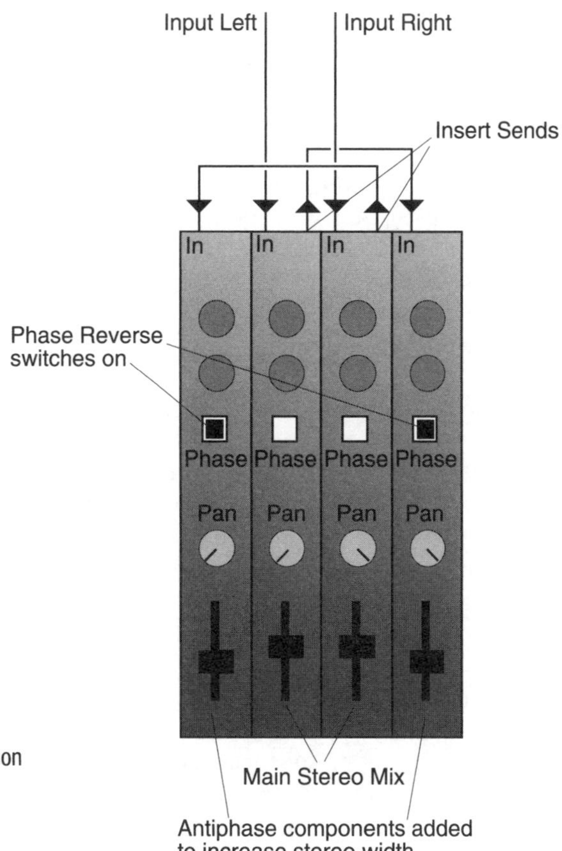

Figure 15.5: Stereo Width Expansion

the only changes will be changes in perceived level. Figure 15.5 shows how the stereo width expansion trick works.

Difficult Mixes

If you can't get a mix sounding right, check the following points:

◆ Try to get an initial rough mix without using EQ or effects and then work from there. Also check that the mix sounds OK in mono.

◆ Is there too much going on at once? Do you need all those parts, and if so, can some of them afford to be lower in the mix?

◆ Are mid-range sounds cluttering up the mix or overlapping with the bass sounds? If so, try using EQ to thin out the sounds. They might sound odd in isolation but they are more likely to sound right in the context of the whole mix. For example, shave some bottom end off a pad synth part or acoustic guitar rhythm line to clean up the low-mid region of the mix.

◆ If you are still having difficulty, balance up the drum and bass sounds first and then add the vocals and main instruments. You will probably find that the mix sounds 90% there with just the drums, bass, chords and a vocal line.

◆ If you are working with a sequencer, try alternative pad or keyboard sounds if the sounds you have chosen appear to be taking up too much space.

◆ Use effects sparingly — add reverb where it sounds good, not simply where you feel it ought to be. Very often the restrained use of effects produces the best result.

◆ Pan the instruments and effects to their desired positions.

◆ There may be some benefit in adding a little compression to the complete mix, though this shouldn't be considered compulsory. A compressor with an auto attack/release feature may cope best with the shifting dynamics of a real mix, and a soft-knee expander will usually provide the most transparent results.

◆ Valve compressors often give the most flattering sound, and many top engineers like to pass the mix through their favourite valve compressor more for the benefit of the valve coloration than for the compression.

◆ Subtle use of an enhancer such as an Aural Exciter will also help separate the individual sounds and emphasise detail.

chapter 16

a tapeless future?

Put simply, tapeless recording is the process of recording digitised audio data to a hard disk drive or other suitable data storage system rather than using conventional tape. Such digital recording systems can be used in place of conventional multitrack recorders, they can be used to edit existing stereo material, or they may be used to edit sound samples prior to transferring the results to a conventional MIDI sampler. Perhaps the most attractive aspect of hard disk recording is that it can be integrated into a MIDI sequencing package to provide a complete music recording solution at a relatively low cost.

The large capacity hard disk drives required to store audio data were originally prohibitively expensive, but that's no longer the case. Indeed, it can only be a matter of time before disk storage is actually cheaper than buying professional audio tape. Even at current prices, hard disk recording is well within reach of even the most casual computer owning audio enthusiast and is becoming more affordable by the month.

The cost of removable media, primarily magnetic and magneto-optical drive cartridges, is also falling dramatically, while speed and capacity continue to increase, and though backing up large files cost-effectively is a significant problem at the moment (excepting slow data DAT backup), the time will soon come when we can record directly to an archiving medium that's as affordable and as convenient as tape. CD-R is already a viable and relatively cheap alternative for archiving completed projects, its only drawback being that the recorded data cannot be changed.

Hardware Formats

The majority of tapeless recording systems use computer hard disks, but you don't have to use a desktop computer in order to record digitally. Though computer-based systems are invariably the most flexible, they also tend to be quite complicated and even the best systems crash inexplicably from time to time. Those wanting to avoid the computer route can choose from hardware workstations, which may offer recording and mixing combined in a single package, or stand-alone disk-based multitracks that replace conventional multitrack tape machines. Already such machines are cheaper than their tape-based counterparts and are commonly available in 4-, 8- or 16-track versions.

Stereo material sampled at 44.1kHz (the same as CD), uses around 10Mbytes of disk space per minute, which means around 600Mbytes of disk space is needed to store an hour's worth of stereo material. In practice though, you need rather more, because if you decide to do a destructive edit, the system usually creates backup files so that you can change your mind if things don't work out. This being the case, a 1Gbyte drive should be considered the bare minimum for a typical album project with 2Gbytes being preferable.

For multitracking, the recording time is halved every time you double the number of tracks, so using the same 600Mbyte drive, you get about 15 minutes of continuous 8-track recording time or less than eight minutes of 16-track recording. It's also worth noting that larger capacity drives (2Gbytes and over), tend to be faster making them more suitable for multitracking. In multitracking applications, it is important to choose a fast AV drive so that fast, continuous data transfer rates can be sustained.

Random Access

Unlike recordings made onto tape, audio data on hard disk can be accessed very rapidly without the need to rewind. Even sections of recording that are, say, half an hour apart can be accessed in milliseconds, and with the addition of a little buffer memory plus suitable editing software, it is possible to select sections from anywhere on the disk and replay these in any order with absolutely no break between them. This so-called random access is fundamental to hard disk editing, and it makes possible editing procedures that were quite unthinkable by conventional means. Furthermore, the original recorded data need never be erased or altered – the editing is non-destructive. In order to prevent clicks at the edit points, most software creates a brief crossfade at each edit point.

The way in which a hard disk editing unit handles data will be more readily appreciated by those who have had some experience with MIDI sequencers. A sequencer allows a composition to be built up by combining various sections or patterns into some kind of order, and there is no restriction on how many times the same pattern can be used. For example, a chorus section can be recorded as a pattern and then called up whenever a chorus is required. Hard disk random access allows us to do exactly the same with audio data. Songs can be divided into sections such as verses, choruses, intros, links, bridges, solos and so on, then rearranged to produce a longer or more interesting version of the song.

Audio Quality

16-bit hard disk recording has the potential to provide the same audio quality as CD, but in practice, the fidelity is limited by the quality of the D to A and A to D converter chips and the circuits they are used in. For example, high quality converters in an external rack box are capable of producing truly professional results, whereas budget converters residing in a computer, either as part of the basic hardware or as sound cards, are much more likely to pick up noise from the computer's own electronics. They may also use lower cost converter chips which offer relatively poor resolution resulting in increased noise and distortion.

How audio gets into your system depends on the hardware you have – budget sound cards tend to have analogue inputs and outputs only, while more sophisticated systems have S/PDIF and or AES/EBU digital interfaces as well. Computers with on-board audio capability are usually fitted with mini jacks, RCA phono jacks or other non professional connectors to carry the audio. If the digital inputs and outputs are used, then the recording quality is limited mainly by the performance of the converters used in the DAT machine or other external device first used to digitise the audio.

Analogue recordings are fine for multitrack work because most of the source material is analogue – all you need do is take line outs from a mixer – but for editing stereo material, it's generally considered unacceptable to leave the digital domain unless you need to process the audio using an analogue process such as an esoteric equaliser. Normally, the data to be edited is fed in from DAT or another digital source via the digital I/O connectors, and it's wise to use a proper digital transfer cable – the impedance is different to that of audio cable. Though it's sometimes possible to get away with using a regular hi-fi RCA phono lead as a digital cable, you might just end up with clicks and glitches which you can't explain.

For serious applications, systems based on external hardware offer better audio performance and interfaces with multiple ins and outs are available for multitrack work – particularly important if you intend to use a conventional analogue mixer to mix and process the individual tracks. Current examples of multiple output computer-based systems include Digidesign's Pro Tools III/IV or Session 8. Pro Tools is a particularly interesting system because it can be expanded to form a complete virtual studio environment complete with multitrack recording, automated mixing and plug-in, software-based effects and signal processors. With the shift towards the PC as the standard computing platform, especially in the cost-conscious entry level market (previously, the Mac was the accepted audio platform), there will no doubt be a number of competitively priced new systems coming onto the market in the very near future.

A well designed 16-bit, 44.1kHz or 48kHz linear sampling system is comparable in audio quality to CD, though some low cost systems use data compression to allow more tracks to be recorded onto limited disk space. Although the best of these systems are very good, all forms of data compression have some adverse effect on the fidelity of the signal in much the same way as noise reduction systems affect the integrity of analogue recordings. MiniDisk uses its own data compression system and achieves near CD quality while storing only around a quarter of the data that would be needed for uncompressed audio. Several MiniDisk-based 4-track systems are currently available aimed at the top end of the existing Portastudio market.

For professional recording and editing, systems without any form of data compression are much preferred, though compressed audio will certainly play an important part in multimedia work where data rates are important. Many radio stations already use MiniDisk to compile programmes or as 'cart' replacements for jingles and commercials.

Stand-Alone Recorders

Anyone not entirely comfortable with computers might prefer to go for a stand-alone digital recorder. At the very least, this should sidestep any compatibility issues, though there's no guarantee that stand-alone systems won't crash from time to time. Hard disk or MiniDisk-based digital recorders range upwards in price from as little as a serious cassette multitracker, and the reason prices have fallen so significantly is that, unlike analogue recording, the hardware is based on the same generic components used elsewhere in the computer industry.

A number of stand-alone hard disk recorders are currently available with multiple inputs and outputs, and there's a trend to give these machines controls similar to those found on a traditional tape machine. The sound quality of stand-alone systems is again dictated by the quality of converters used and by the circuitry that supports them.

Many stand-alone, tapeless multitrackers are designed to be used with a conventional analogue mixer in exactly the same way as a standard tape machine. The main differences are that there's no waiting time while you rewind, plus you get the benefits of cut, copy and paste editing. The majority of machines will also have synchronisation facilities, either built-in or as optional accessories. These may range from simple MTC or MIDI clock generation to being able to sync to external time code; the latter facility is necessary when slaving recorders to video machines.

Audio On Computers

To record audio on a computer, you need to add a suitable audio interface (unless the computer has 16-bit audio capability), software and usually an external hard drive. The hardware can be as simple as a sound card or it could be an external rack box of A/D and D/A converters with multiple input and output capability. AV Macintosh or Power PC Macintosh computers can record and play back audio using the computer's integral 16-bit sound facility, which means the only additional expense is the software. The main limitation of simple card or AV-based systems is that you can usually only record two audio tracks at one time, and all your audio tracks are mixed to stereo as you play them back.

More sophisticated cards offer additional analogue or digital inputs and there is a move towards software supporting multiple sound cards where greater I/O capacity is required. The better cards also include a degree of DSP capability enabling them to provide effects, EQ or mixing capability without draining the resources of the host computer. However, you can get a feel for hard disk recording using something as simple as a cheap Sound Blaster type games card and then move up to more elaborate hardware when you feel the need. PCI cards are available for both Mac and PC platforms with one or two of the non-mainstream computers also offering some form of audio recording option, most notably the Atari-based Falcon.

Material is recorded onto disk in real time, either from a digital source or as a conventional analogue signal from a mixer, DI box or mic preamp. If the transfer is digital, then the recording is an exact clone of the original and there is no need to worry about recording levels. However, metering is usually provided for level setting when the analogue inputs are used, and in common with other digital systems, clipping occurs as soon as 0dB is exceeded – there's no headroom as there is with analogue tape.

The main editing tasks you can do with digital systems are based around rearranging your material in a different order, but you can also normalise signal levels to bring the peaks up to 0dB, apply digital EQ, reverse sections of sound, create fade-ins and fade-outs and a number of other things which would have been difficult or impossible using tape and razor blades. Some advanced systems allow you to use plug-in, software-based effects such as reverb, delay, compression, noise removal and stereo/3D enhancement, the best of which equal or exceed the capabilities of their hardware equivalents.

Media Costs

Even at today's low prices for hard and removable drives, the cost of leaving material archived on your drive is high – and this applies to both computer-based and stand-alone systems. Every track-minute of 16-bit audio sampled at 44.1kHz eats up around 5Mbytes of disk space, which means an album project recorded over 24 tracks might take up around 10Gbytes of disk space. One option is to back up your data to a tape-based data backup system such as Exobyte or a DAT data backup device. Backing up to digital tape in this way is very time consuming, but the huge saving in cost makes it worth the inconvenience for non-time-sensitive projects.

Even the most reliable systems occasionally suffer computer crashes, and though you can normally restart the computer and carry on, there are times when a crash will corrupt some or all of your data on disk, so if you haven't made a backup, your work is as good as lost. A very wise person once said that digital data doesn't really exist until you have it stored in at least two different places. Anyone moving into tapeless recording must develop a 'back up mentality' if disaster is to be averted.

Hard Disk Editors

Hard disk editors exist specifically to manipulate and rearrange stereo material, and their most common musical applications involve compiling individual tracks to produce a Production Master tape for an album project or to chop up and move the various sections of a song so as to create a new arrangement. This technique is often used to create extended remixes for twelve inch release or to shorten songs. Sophisticated crossfading algorithms are used to ensure that there are no audible glitches at the edit points – something that isn't always true when editing analogue tape using razor blades! Editing is also frequently employed to assemble the best parts of several different takes or versions of the same song. Some editors also double as sample editors and communicate with MIDI samplers either via MIDI (which is very slow), or via SCSI. Other applications include compiling soundtracks for games, multimedia products, TV sound and even film soundtracks.

Album Compiling

When compiling an album, the required songs are recorded into the system either via the analogue inputs or via a direct digital S/PDIF link from a DAT machine. If the original master is digital, then the transfer should be in the digital domain unless a specific analogue process is to be applied during transfer. Editing is accomplished by dividing the recording into

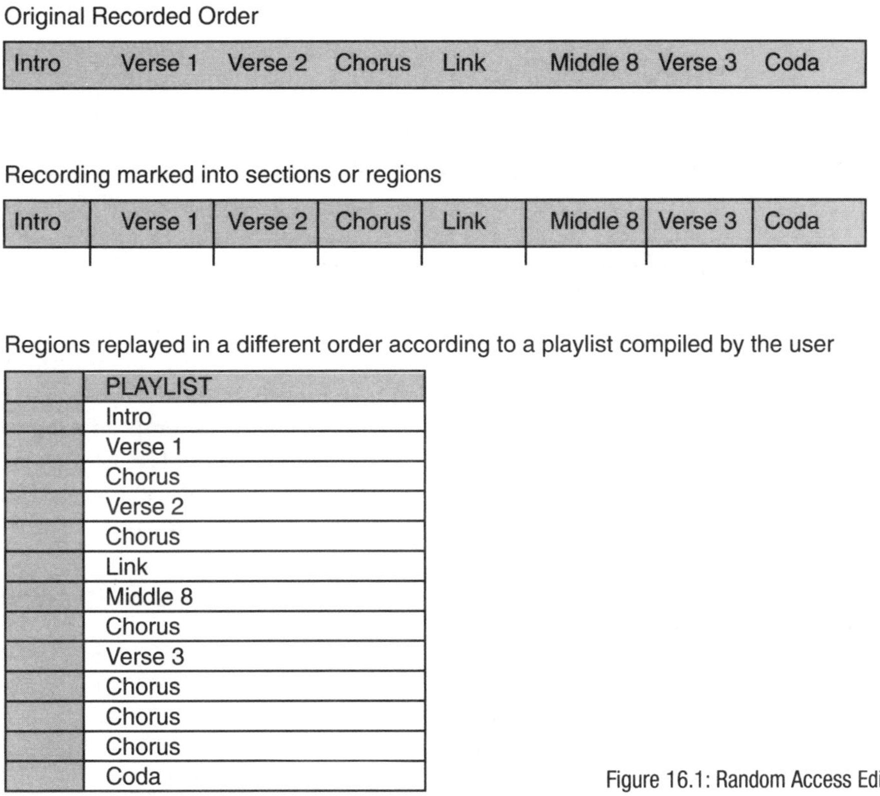

Original Recorded Order

Intro	Verse 1	Verse 2	Chorus	Link	Middle 8	Verse 3	Coda

Recording marked into sections or regions

Intro	Verse 1	Verse 2	Chorus	Link	Middle 8	Verse 3	Coda

Regions replayed in a different order according to a playlist compiled by the user

	PLAYLIST
	Intro
	Verse 1
	Chorus
	Verse 2
	Chorus
	Link
	Middle 8
	Chorus
	Verse 3
	Chorus
	Chorus
	Chorus
	Coda

Figure 16.1: Random Access Editing

marked sections which can then be compiled into a playlist. Indeed, many so-called extended remixes are accomplished using these techniques and a typical remix application is shown in Figure 16.1.

Some systems allow cue points to be set 'on the fly', making it very easy to mark a song at exactly the right place. The edit points can be subsequently fine-tuned to eliminate any remaining timing errors. This degree of precision is very useful when it comes to removing unwanted sounds that occur before the start of a song, such as count-in beats or the noise of fingers on guitar strings.

The individual songs simply have their start and end points marked, and are then arranged in the correct order with the required gap between each. Most computer-based systems provide some form of visual display showing the audio waveform of the material being worked on; this makes it easier to locate the starts and ends of songs. It is normally possible to audition the transition between one song and the next, and if the gap is too short or too long, it can easily be modified. Fade-outs at the end of songs can be handled automatically by marking the start and end of the fade, while some systems allow the respective levels of different marked sections to be adjusted and may provide some form of digital equalisation. These latter two facilities can be invaluable when compiling songs from different recording sessions to go on the same album. With a little effort, their levels and tonal balances can be matched to give a more cohesive result. However, not all hard disk editing systems have all the aforementioned features.

Album compilation is pretty routine stuff to a digital editing system, but it does offer far greater precision than manual editing methods and, once the songs have been marked and named, it is easy to compile several alternative running orders, as might be necessary when producing masters for CD, vinyl and cassette releases of the same album. Live albums may also be assembled using the best takes from several performances, and here, the ability to crossfade between sections of audience ambience or applause is invaluable in creating a seamless end product.

Rearranging

It is when editing individual songs that the real power of a digital hard disk editor becomes apparent. Providing the recorded material is accurately marked off into sections, these can be strung together with no trace of a glitch between them. A straight butt joint between sections is normally quite satisfactory, but the better editors offer crossfading between sections for occasions where this is more appropriate. It is normally best to choose edit points that coincide with drum beats, as these make timing easy to handle and tend to hide any discontinuities that might occur when joining two sections which weren't originally consecutive.

Destructive Editing

As touched upon earlier in the chapter, random access allows you to call up any piece of data almost instantaneously; you can rearrange the sections of your recording and play them back in any order. Being able to rearrange, copy or remove material in a non-destructive way is very reassuring, but there are times when you may want a change to become permanent – for example, when erasing unwanted noise immediately prior to the start of a song or when normalising the level of a piece of recorded audio. On a computer-based system, you may even be able to zoom in on the audio waveform to wipe out any annoying little guitar squeaks or similar noises with pinpoint accuracy.

While basic cut and paste editing is possible on virtually any multitrack hard disk system, a dedicated stereo editing system or software package will usually include specialist tools that can be used to edit to a much finer degree. For example, Digidesign's Sound Designer software lets you use an on-screen pen tool to redraw small sections of the waveform, which can be a life saver if you find a short glitch or click in the middle of your master tape. Third party software plug-ins providing compression, limiting, EQ, noise reduction, noise-shaped dithering, stereo image correction and three-dimensional sound processing may all be used destructively to create a new file containing the changed data. However, providing you have enough free disk space, even destructive edits aren't usually irrevocable because your original file remains intact allowing you to undo whatever edit you last did. If spare disk space is low, you should see a warning message telling you that you won't be able to undo the operation you're currently considering.

Corrective Measures

Some computer-based systems allow the operator to zoom right in on a tiny section of the musical waveform, where flaws such as interference clicks can be identified quite easily. These can usually be 'drawn out' using an on-screen drawing tool to replace the damaged section with something smoother or, alternatively, a similar section can be copied from elsewhere in the song and pasted in the place of the damaged piece. This is not always as easy as it seems, but an experienced operator should be able to cope with most eventualities. There are also plug-in software modules for some systems that facilitate noise removal, click removal and even crackle removal, the latter being used for restoring vinyl recordings.

Where a section of audio is damaged beyond restoration, it is sometimes possible to find a similar phrase from elsewhere in the song, or even from within a completely different take of the song, and then paste that in place of the faulty section using crossfading to disguise the join.

Time/pitch compression or expansion is also made possible using sophisticated software routines, and because the process can be carried out off-line as opposed to in real time, more processing power can be brought to bear. This usually produces results that are noticeably superior to what you might expect from a rack-mount pitch shifter. By treating only selected sections of audio, out of tune notes can be brought back to pitch, a slightly slow section copied from an out-take can be matched with the tempo of the current version and so on.

A relatively recent innovation is the use of format-corrected pitch shifting, which can be used either to increase the amount of pitch shift that may be applied before the voice or instrument starts to sound unnatural or, alternatively, the character of a voice or instrument may be changed without altering its pitch.

Audio With MIDI

The most affordable way to get into tapeless recording is to add audio to your MIDI sequencer. Anything you record can be accessed and manipulated in much the same way as you arrange your sequenced MIDI patterns, and you only pay out for one computer. If you do most of your work with MIDI already, then adding a few tracks of hard disk audio is a very practical and flexible way to upgrade and avoids the need to synchronise a tape system to a MIDI sequencer. Because a typical MIDI composition may only include a small amount of audio – perhaps vocals and the odd guitar part – removable media drives become more cost effective as a storage medium.

Currently, most of the leading sequencer manufacturers are including basic audio capability in their standard software packages – you only have to pay for the audio version if you want to work with more sophisticated, multichannel hardware. To take advantage of the audio recording facility, you need an AV Mac, a Power Macintosh with 16-bit audio support or either a PC or Mac fitted with a suitable sound card.

The full audio versions of these programs tend to support third-party hardware such as Digidesign's Pro Tools III/IV system, which allows the use of multiple software plug-ins to create a virtual studio environment complete with comprehensive mixing and automation routines.

Tapeless Workstations

Hard disk recorders require DSP power to process data, so by adding more DSP power, it's possible to add digital mixing and real-time signal processing. This makes your system a computer-based workstation rather than simply a recorder. In the case of Digidesign's Pro Tools III/IV systems, additional DSP cards are fitted inside the computer, and by using their proprietary TDM buss, data can be routed round the system very quickly. This makes it possible to create a complete recording and mixing environment where the only practical limit to performance is the amount of DSP power plugged in.

Hardware equivalent systems have been available for some time and are used extensively in the film, video and post pro markets. Lower cost models for musicians' use may have fewer functions, but they still offer far more flexibility and better audio quality than traditional tape-based solutions. Low cost digital workstations are encroaching on the market once dominated by the cassette multitrack studio and the combination of digital multitrack, automated digital mixing and on-board effects is very appealing, especially for the musician who may need only limited editing capabilities.

At the budget end of the scale, MiniDisk is being pressed into service as an affordable replacement for the traditional cassette multitracker, though on all the models seen so far, the mixer section is based on traditional analogue circuitry. Though actually more costly per track than a true 16-bit linear hard disk solution, MiniDisk has the advantage of relatively low media costs, which avoids the need for time consuming backup routines. Stand-alone systems have the disadvantage that you can't generally use third-party software, but the fact that they have a dedicated user interface can make them less confusing than mouse and keyboard-driven systems.

Looking further into the future, we'll probably see more computer-based, direct-to-disk systems connected to dedicated hardware control surfaces to make them feel more like using a conventional mixer and recorder. Already there are surprisingly inexpensive hardware systems offering friendly user interfaces, but dedicated control surfaces for computer systems are traditionally expensive. However, as the feature list continues to expand, a time will come when it is no longer practical to control an entire system via a single mouse and a number of traditional mixer companies are already looking closely at the control surface marketplace.

Card-based systems are also likely to grow to a point where standard computers can no longer contain all the cards a user may wish to use, and the situation will be made more acute by the continuing introduction of high quality MIDI synthesizers on cards. It seems likely that the sophisticated system of the future will use a computer as a front end, but the converters, DSP cards, synthesizer cards and so on will be located in an external hardware rack or expansion chassis.

Practicalities

If you're running a hard disk recording system on a computer, with or without external hardware, it is always better to use a separate drive to store your audio. The reason being that audio drives need to be emptied or defragmented pretty regularly (using Norton Utilities or similar software), and if you have all your other software and system files residing on the same drive, this becomes more difficult. With a separate drive, all you need do is back up the project, then trash all the data on the drive ready to start a new session.

One area of concern when transferring from DAT in the digital domain is that any errors caused by interference picking up on the cable can give rise to seemingly inexplicable clicks or glitches on the finished master. It is therefore imperative that good quality cable and connectors are used and that the cable is kept as short as possible. It is also wise to use a mains filtering system to avoid mains-borne interference causing data corruption.

As touched upon earlier in the chapter, it is advisable to choose a hard drive specified for AV use. Conventional hard drives take occasional short brakes for auto thermal recalibration, which can cause dropouts in the audio, especially when multiple tracks are being recorded or played back. AV drives, on the other hand, have an intelligent recalibration system that only operates when the drive isn't recording or playing data.

To be safe, it's always best to check with the manufacturer of your digital audio system which drives have been approved as compatible. When you start to mix audio and computers, you can end up with all kinds of inexplicable compatibility problems that are very difficult to solve. You even need to check that your choice of system will work with the model of computer that you have or are thinking of buying. If there is a problem, and you didn't buy the entire system from one dealer, there's a good chance that everyone concerned will claim their part of the system is OK and there's very little you can do about it.

Continuing Progress

The future certainly belongs to tapeless recording, and presumably, in the longer term, solid-state rather than disk storage, but until we get a data storage solution that's as cheap as tape, digital tape backup systems such as Data DAT, look like having a secure future. Furthermore, recording onto tape, either analogue or digital, has the overriding advantage of low cost and simplicity of operation. With most tapeless systems, work has to be backed up in order to free up the disk for the next project. Backing up is very time consuming and even the faster digital tape-based systems are not significantly faster than real time when backing up stereo recordings.

For multitrack recording, the problem is compounded – working in real time, one hour of 16-track recording would take eight hours to back up and a further eight hours to reload (time based on eight stereo pairs). Until inexpensive, removable disk media become available, tape and disk will tend to be used alongside each other so that the strengths of each format may be utilised to the full.

Analogue Or Digital Recording

You can easily get the impression that the 'analogue versus digital recording' question has escalated almost into a religious war, but the reality of the situation is that both technologies offer clear advantages in specific areas. Though this chapter deviates somewhat from the main thrust of this book, I feel that it is important to look at the pros and cons of both analogue and digital recording formats so that you can decide which technology is most suitable for a specific project.

Until the early 90s, the predominant professional recording medium was analogue tape. Though it probably wasn't realised at the time, the analogue tape recorder is unique in that it was one of the few mass-produced systems developed specifically for audio recording. This is in contrast to many digital recording systems, which utilise computer, video and hi-fi technology to make manufacture commercially viable. For example, DAT (Digital Audio Tape recorder), is a hi-fi spinoff owing much to the mechanics of the video recorder, R-DAT (Rotary head, Digital Audio Tape recorder), multitracks use video technology (and video tapes), while hard disk recorders depend on general purpose computer hardware. Only very expensive and very specialised open-reel digital tape machines are designed from the ground up purely to satisfy the needs of the audio industry.

Analogue recording has been refined over the past few decades to a point that it is unlikely that any further significant improvements will be made, especially as the declining market makes it more difficult to fund further development. Indeed, Dolby SR noise reduction may well be the last major hardware breakthrough, along with the recent introduction of high energy tapes helping snatch a few more dB of dynamic range. By using the latest generation of tapes alongside Dolby SR noise reduction, analogue recorders can provide a dynamic range approaching that of 16-bit digital recorders while providing adequate headroom to accommodate unexpected transients. What's more, unlike other noise reduction systems, Dolby SR has virtually no audible side effects.

For all the technical improvements, analogue tape still exhibits a magnetic saturation effect when overloaded, which results in a progressive increase in distortion at higher recording levels. This 'flaw', however, is largely responsible for the psychoacoustic warmth and energy of analogue recording. Top engineers often like to use analogue tape either at the multitracking or mastering stage purely because of its subjective sound (and sometimes because of its reliability), but this raises the question – if analogue multitrack is so great, why consider using anything else?

Disadvantages Of Tape

Any tape recorder, analogue or digital, suffers from the inherent disadvantage that the tape is in physical contact with the heads and guides of the machine, which means friction causes deterioration to both the tape itself, and to the heads and tape guides of the recorder. The other obvious disadvantage of tape is that winding the tape from one spool to another takes time, even though in the case of DAT, and some other digital formats, the wind speed is very high.

While the best analogue machines can sound excellent on both a technical and artistic level, the actual results obtained are dependent on the electronic design of the recorder, the mechanics of the transport and the quality of the tape being used. If the tape is not moved across the heads at a perfectly constant speed, then undesirable effects such as wow and flutter become evident. Solo piano is a good test for wow and flutter – because it has no natural vibrato, any speed fluctuations are clearly audible.

Analogue machines also suffer from modulation noise, sometimes called 'bias bubble', caused by the way the magnetic field is disturbed as the tape moves over the surface of the head. If you record a pure sine wave and then play it back, you'll hear a disturbing 'granular' sounding jitter, and though this is seldom audible with normal audio material, it can compromise the quality of solo flute recordings or other instruments that produce a very pure, sustained tone. All analogue machines suffer from this problem, yet perform the same test on a digital machine and the test tone will come out as pure as it went in.

Tape Speed

With a well set up, properly designed analogue tape machine, the most significant factors affecting sound quality are tape speed and track width. The general rule is that the faster the tape passes over the heads and the wider the tracks (the tape width itself is immaterial), the lower the noise and distortion. Narrow format open-reel machines and cassette multitrack systems can't produce an adequately low noise floor without some help from noise reduction systems, and all noise reduction systems cause some degree of deterioration in other aspects of the sound quality. For this reason, professionals tend to prefer working with two inch multitrack tape running at 30ips without noise reduction, and where noise reduction must be used, Dolby SR is by far the best. For mastering use, half inch tape running at 30ips without noise reductions is usually considered to be the best option.

Cassette multitrackers have particularly narrow tracks, and even the models that run at double the normal cassette speed are still four times slower than an open reel machine running at 15 ips. Because of these limitations, cassette multitrackers are all equipped with noise reduction, though the actual system depends on the manufacturer. The better machines now offer Dolby S noise reduction which is a sophisticated consumer system based on some of the principles of both Dolby SR and Dolby C.

Noise Reduction

This section isn't intended to provide an in-depth insight into the workings of the different noise reduction systems, rather to offer means of comparing them in terms of the amount of noise reduction that can be obtained. Equally as important, the side-effects produced by the various systems are described.

Noise reduction systems were devised to reduce the amount of tape noise in analogue tape recording systems, and one thing they all have in common is that some process is applied on recording while the inverse process is applied during playback. For this reason, all these systems are all known as encode/decode systems. How well the process is implemented determines what audible side-effects are produced. These systems reduce the effect of tape hiss but have no effect on any noise inherent in the signal being recorded.

dbx

dbx is most often used in cassette multitrackers and works by compressing the audio with a 2:1 ratio during recording and then expanding it with the same ratio during playback. There's also an element of high frequency pre-emphasis/de-emphasis employed to further minimise high frequency noise. This approach results in the greatest improvement in signal-to-noise ratio, but it also has the most serious side-effects, especially when used on budget cassette systems. One such effect is 'noise pumping' or 'breathing' where some background hiss can be heard over the top of bass sounds that don't have enough high-frequency content to hide the noise. This stems from the fact that all noise reduction systems rely on the wanted signal to mask the noise during loud passages, but because dbx is a fairly simple compression/expansion system, there are occasions on which loud sounds don't contain enough HF to cover the hiss. For example, a solo bass guitar might reveal noise behind the signal, even though the pauses between notes remain quiet.

A dynamic range in excess of 90dB can be achieved with dbx, but in practice, noise from other sources, such as mic amps and instruments is far more significant than tape hiss when you get down to this level. A little additional noise is usually preferable to noise pumping or compressed dynamics which is why some users have a preference for Dolby. When using dbx, it is not recommended that you drive the record level meters into the red because the effect of tape compression will be magnified by the expander circuit in the decoder, producing a choked sound.

Dolby

Dolby NR systems operate in quite a different way to compander systems like dbx. Dolby take the approach that as only low-level signals are likely to be affected by noise, the louder signals can be left unprocessed. Where noise is naturally masked by the program material, little or no processing takes place, but where either the level or spectral content of the program makes it vulnerable to noise, then the noise reduction circuitry comes into play.

Dolby A

Dolby A has been around since the early days of multitrack recording and is only ever found in professional recording systems, never in consumer machines. The system works on selective pre-emphasis, but splits the audio signal into four separate frequency bands (three shelving and one bandpass), each of which is processed independently and then added back to the original, untreated signal. The main benefit of using multiple frequency bands is that high level sounds occupying only a narrow band within the audio spectrum don't compromise the amount of noise reduction being applied to the remaining bands. The maximum amount of available noise reduction is quite modest, being about 15dB (and only 10dB below 5kHz), but the multi-band approach introduces fewer side-effects than the simpler domestic systems.

Dolby B And C

The original Dolby B- and C-type processes are sliding-band systems originally designed for use in consumer cassette machines where high frequency noise or tape hiss is the main problem. They adjust their processing according to the high frequency content of the programme being treated so that noise reduction is only applied when the HF content is inadequate to mask the noise. The net result is that quiet, high frequency signals are recorded louder onto tape, then on playback, they are restored to their correct level. This has the effect of reducing the audible tape noise, though it obviously has no effect on noise which is recorded as part of the original signal. With Dolby B the HF boost on encode (record), is 10dB which gives a corresponding subjective improvement of 10dB in high frequency tape noise.

Dolby C-type processing can be thought of as two Dolby B-type circuits working at different levels, one stage feeding straight into the next. On record, very low-level HF will be boosted twice giving an improvement in signal-to-noise of 20dB at frequencies above 1kHz, which is where most audible hiss occurs.

Dolby SR

Dolby SR is Dolby's flagship noise reduction system and was introduced at around the time digital recording really took off in an attempt to give the analogue recorder a longer lease of life. In excess of 25dB of noise reduction is possible with minimal side-effects, but Dolby SR is technically quite complicated and hence costly. Unlike previous Dolby systems which operated on the 'if it ain't broke, don't fix it' principle by treating only low level sounds, Dolby SR tries to ensure that the maximum possible energy is recorded in all frequency bands all the time. To do this, SR employs ten filters, some with fixed frequency bands and others that slide to cover different parts of the spectrum depending on the characteristics of the programme material. This means the system has to do some pretty complex analysis of the input signal in real time, and the decoding process is equally complicated. Anti-saturation measures are employed to prevent HF tape overload.

Dolby SR enables analogue recordings to rival the best digital recordings as far as noise and dynamic range are concerned, and as an additional benefit, it is reasonably tolerant of level errors or tape speed changes, which means a degree of varispeed may be used without ruining the sound. Because of the high cost, Dolby SR is only found in professional systems, usually in the form of an add-on rack system or as plug in cards.

Dolby S

The newer Dolby S, designed for high-end consumer recorders, might appear complex by comparison with Dolby B and C, but it uses only half as many processing bands as Dolby SR. In fact Dolby S uses two principles from SR, the first being Action Substitution – a combination of fixed and sliding filter bands that provide a more adaptive response to the signal spectrum. The second, Modulation Control, uses extra control signals to prevent high level signals in one area compromising the noise reduction in other parts of the audio spectrum.

Dolby S combines aspects from both Dolby C and SR to produce better than 10dB improvement at extreme high frequencies, 24dB of noise reduction above 400Hz and 10dB of NR below 200Hz. Finally, because Dolby S is so much less complex than SR, it can be built into a single IC for use in consumer audio products.

In practical terms, Dolby S offers extra headroom at both high and low frequencies, giving the semi professional multitrack running high energy tape a dynamic range approaching 90dB. It has already been adopted by both Fostex and Tascam for use in their project studio analogue multitrack machines with great success, largely because the audible side effects are far less than for other consumer systems. Other than areas such as wow and flutter (which noise reduction systems don't purport to address), the audio quality from semi-pro analogue machines now rivals that of 16-bit digital multitrack with the further benefit of analogue 'warmth' when the tape is driven hard.

On a high quality machine, Dolby B typically produces a dynamic range in excess of 65dB, Dolby C typically produces a dynamic range in excess of 75dB, while Dolby S and SR can push this figure to in excess of 82dB, though the actual figure will depend on whether normal or high energy tape is being used and on the technical performance of the recorder itself.

Dolby HX Pro is not a noise reduction system in its own right but rather a system for reducing the risk of tape saturation at high frequencies. HX Pro is normally used in conjunction with other Dolby Noise Reduction systems and is often found on domestic hi-fi cassette decks.

Analogue Copying

When an analogue recording is copied from one tape track to another during track bouncing, some loss of quality is inevitable. At every stage of copying, more noise is added and a little more clarity is lost. There can also be problems when playing back tapes recorded on different machines due to small differences in the mechanical head alignment. Alignment problems are most likely to manifest themselves as a loss of high frequencies or a change in levels. There's also the question of whether the original tape was recorded on a machine with IEC or NAB equalisation, and playing back with the wrong equalisation will cause a tonal change.

Analogue recording has well-documented technical weaknesses, but the benefits are still very worthwhile. Analogue tape recorders have been around for a long time; they work, they're not too difficult to maintain, and tape itself is relatively cheap when you compare it with hard disk or removable disk systems. The tape can spliced, which makes basic editing easy, and recordings can be kept for many years with minimal deterioration providing they are stored in a suitable environment. Recordings that have deteriorated due to 'sticky shed syndrome' can usually be made playable again by baking overnight at 50 degrees C in a temperature-controlled oven or incubator.

Because you can overdrive analogue tape without getting into hard clipping, you can be a little more casual about recording levels than you have to be with digital systems. Digital systems simply clip, and unless the periods of clipping are extremely short, the result is generally audible as an unpleasant crackle or glitch. Other analogue advantages, when it comes to creativity, are that you can varispeed analogue tape over a very large range, you can even turn the tape over to create reverse effects. Two analogue machines may be used to create flanging by playing back two copies of the same recording, then using your hand as a brake on one or other of the machine's tape reels so that the timing between the two machines wanders slightly.

If you do experience a problem with an analogue tape, such as dropout (usually caused by faulty tape or large pieces of foreign material on the heads), you can hear the problem straight away and either redo the recording on a new tape or try to patch in a piece copied from elsewhere in the song. Any further deterioration caused by inappropriate storage is usually gradual and generally involves an overall loss of quality rather than a drastic and complete failure.

Digital Tape

There's a lot of rhetoric about the way digital recordings sound, but ultimately, most serious music listening is done via Compact Disk, a 16-bit digital format with a theoretical maximum dynamic range of 96dB. This figure is considerably better than you can get from most analogue recording systems, even with noise reduction, but you have to keep in mind that digital systems have no headroom at all above 0VU – there's no soft clipping as there is with analogue tape. When working with digital multitrack, it may be necessary to set the nominal record level at around -12dB on the recorder's own meters to prevent the peaks from clipping. Once you've allowed a little safety headroom, a 16-bit digital system probably has little more usable dynamic range than a good analogue recorder working with Dolby SR. However, dynamic range isn't the only issue.

All digital recording systems work by sampling the instantaneous level of the input signal, usually at either 44,100 or 48,000 times a second, then storing these samples as binary numbers. The number of bits used to represent a sample defines the precision or resolution of the analogue-to-digital conversion process – the fewer the number of bits, the lower the accuracy. Because every sample is measured to the nearest bit, the digital representation of an analogue waveform is really a series of tiny steps, and in the case of a 16-bit system, a full-scale signal would occupy two to the power of 16 or 65,536 steps. If the signal being recorded is large, it will use most of the available bits and so be adequately accurate, but smaller signals will be represented by fewer bits. This means that the lower the signal level, the higher the percentage of distortion.

Analogue machines work the other way round – the distortion increases as the level increases, but because tape distortion is mainly second harmonic, small amounts actually flatter the sound, which is one reason so many people prefer working with analogue machines.

Because digital recording introduces no distortions or colorations other than those imposed by the limitations of the quantisation process and by the accuracy of the analogue to digital converters, it's probably reasonable to say that digital systems are more accurate than analogue tape recorders. Recording a pure 1kHz square wave onto both digital and analogue machines, then comparing the output signals on an oscilloscope will prove this point quite dramatically. Indeed, the analogue waveform may be unrecognisable as ever having been a square wave.

A further benefit of digital systems is that no noise reduction is needed, and, because digital machines are crystal controlled, there's no mechanism by which unwanted pitch modulation can be introduced. Even with a budget digital system, wow and flutter is effectively eliminated because the digital data goes to and from tape via a crystal-clocked memory buffer – the input isn't recorded directly to the tape. Once a recording is in the digital domain, it's just a list of numbers, which means you can theoretically copy the data from one digital machine to another or from track to track simply by duplicating these numbers. The result should be a perfect copy with no quality loss.

Error Correction

In practice, the shortcomings of tape can mean that a few of the numbers occasionally get lost or altered during recording or playback. To get around this potentially serious problem, powerful error correction systems are employed to reconstruct damaged data with no loss of accuracy, providing the degree of data corruption is minor. A system of recording redundant data enables the machine to verify the data integrity by means of checksums, and small errors can be repaired completely by using the redundant data to reconstruct the original data. This works because the recording process distributes the data along the tape in such a way that a brief dropout in one place causes a multitude of small errors over a short period of time; if the data were to be recorded linearly, a single dropout would be unrecoverable because all the errors would be in one place. Such error correction systems are vitally important to offset the destructive effects of particles of dirt on the tape's surface and to compensate for minor tape dropouts.

In the case of larger errors, where it isn't possible to reconstruct the original data completely, the system estimates the missing data by a process of interpolation – this is called error concealment. Very large errors, on the other hand, may be too great in duration for the system to be able to estimate the missing data, in which case the output will be muted to prevent audible glitching. Using good tape in a well maintained machine, concealment errors should be rare, while muting should never occur.

The ability to make an accurate clone of a digital tape is of immense value when mastering to DAT or when multitracking using a machine such as an ADAT or DA-88, because a second machine will allow you to make safety copies just in case anything should happen to the original. By contrast, a safety copy of an analogue tape will always be inferior to the original.

Time Code

Digital machines record a sub-code as part of their data stream acting as an invisible timing grid, allowing the machine's tape counters and locators to relate to the actual recording rather than being driven from the transport mechanics, as is the case in analogue machines. With an analogue machine, tape slip results in the displayed tape position drifting, but with a digital machine this can't happen. The sub-code may be used, via suitable hardware, to generate SMPTE, MIDI Clock or MTC sync signals and, conversely, some DAT machines have the ability to record SMPTE time code within their data structure. Such machines are usually used for film and video work where the audio must be synchronised to picture at a later time.

What Can Go Wrong?

When an analogue recorder goes out of alignment, or if the heads become badly worn, the first symptom is a fall-off in high frequency whereas a damaged tape may result in dropouts – brief but audible drops in level and high end frequency response. By contrast, digital machines deal with absolute numbers, but because some errors are inevitable due to dust on the tape, head ware, tape surface imperfections and so on, their error correction systems are constantly working to ensure the reproduced data is accurate.

As touched upon earlier, error correction systems are capable of restoring a limited amount of corrupted data with complete accuracy, but errors involving a greater amount of data corruption may not leave sufficient information for reconstruction of the original data. At this point, the system moves from error correction mode to error concealment. In effect, the software looks at the data each side of the problem section and uses interpolation to construct a plausible replacement for the missing data. Technically, this will cause a brief rise in distortion, but usually too brief to be audible. If longer errors occur, then the system can't even make a guess as to what's missing so it mutes the audio output until more good data is read in. Obviously, muting errors indicate something is seriously wrong, but up until the point muting errors occur, you may be completely unaware that there is a problem at all.

This means that while error correction is a wonderful ally, it prevents us from seeing problems develop until it is too late. Unfortunately, only very costly professional machines tend to have comprehensive error readout systems, though some of the new budget digital multitrack recorders allow you to enter an error readout mode for test purposes. Unlike analogue, there's no gradual loss of sound quality to warn of impending problems because the error correction hides any problems from you until they're relatively serious – the first you know anything is wrong is when you hear a dropout. Because head-wear or recorder misalignment can cause these problems, it is very important to have digital tape machines serviced every 500 hours or so, even if no problems are apparent.

Alignment

The majority of digital recorders use a rotating head, similar to that in a video machine, to allow them to operate at very low tape speeds. Whereas an analogue machine has to have the heads aligned to produce a flat frequency response, digital machines require tape path adjustment to ensure the tape is, in effect, aligned with the head. Any alignment error will cause the digital data to be corrupted causing the error correction system to work overtime. Serious misalignment will cause the system to fail altogether. Because of the tiny component used in digital machines, and the costly specialised test equipment required to verify alignment, servicing is no longer within the province of the average studio service engineer

Another alignment related problem is inter-machine compatibility, which has been a major irritation to DAT users over the past few years. Most of the time, a DAT tape will play back perfectly well on another machine, but occasionally, a small difference in alignment will cause audible dropouts or glitches. Until a truly professional format replaces DAT, I can't see this problem ever being resolved satisfactorily. Again, it is worth having DAT machines serviced every 500 hours whether you appear to be having problems or not.

Tape Editing

Other than the lack of warning prior to a major failure, digital tape can't be edited using razor blades (with the exception of one or two professional, open-reel digital machines which are claimed to allow cut and splice editing). Editing can be achieved by cloning data from one digital machine to another, but this is time consuming and not everyone has access to two machines. In fact the only really satisfactory way to edit digital material is to use a hard disk editing system. These are discussed in the chapter, Hard Disk Recording.

Synchronisation

Current low cost digital multitrack machines record eight tracks on S-VHS or 8mm cassettes and it is possible to lock multiple machines together to provide more tracks where required. The proprietary sync systems offer sample accuracy lock, but there's invariably a period of a second or two between starting the master machine and the slaves locking to it. This might not seem much, but where you're doing a lot of stop/start works such as when punching in vocal corrections, it can become rather frustrating.

By using the appropriate hardware interface, the Alesis, Fostex, Sony and Tascam digital tape machines can be sync'ed to video for to-picture work, and MTC, SMPTE or MIDI Clock can also be generated via external hardware without having to sacrifice a valuable tape track to time code. This latter facility is very valuable to the large number of people using MIDI sequencers in conjunction with tape. Of course you can still SMPTE stripe one track in the usual way if you don't have the appropriate interface and there is no concern over time code crosstalk as there is with analogue machines.

DCC

Another consumer digital format deserving of mention is the Philips DCC consumer cassette, not the least because it introduces the subject of digital data compression. Data reduction algorithms are used to simplify the audio signal so that it can be represented using far less data than uncompressed audio. DCC uses about one quarter of the data necessary to encode an uncompressed signal and this allows a stereo signal to be recorded onto a special tape cassette using a stationary, multichannel head. This type of recorder is known as S-DAT which stands for Stationary Head Digital Tape Recorder as opposed to R-DAT which stands for Rotating Head Digital Tape Recorder.

The data compression used by DCC means the result is technically inferior to DAT and CD insomuch as data reduction can be shown to have audible side-effects on some types of material. Even so, the side effects are less serious than from most types of semi-pro analogue tape noise reduction systems and most people seem unable to differentiate between DCC and CD on commercial pop music. Those with well-trained ears, on the other hand, may hear a difference on classical music, and some listeners complain of a lack of detail or a reduction in the sense of stereo perspective.

At the time of writing, DCC has failed to make a great impression as a consumer format and for this reason, machines are available at very low prices. Though unsuitable for professional work, they are quite viable for home studio mastering. Portable versions are also available for location sound gathering and for recording samples. The recording from a DCC machine can be digitally transferred to DAT but DCC can't be used for backing up digital data from hard disk recorders because of the data reduction algorithms used.

Digital Tape Or Digital Tapeless?

The choice of non-tape-based digital recorders is expanding all the time, and many of these are less costly than their tape based equivalents. They offer on-board editing facilities, usually based on copy, cut and paste functions, and because a disk-based system can access data anywhere on its surface almost instantaneously, there is no waiting for tape to rewind. In most respects, tapeless recording seems to hold all the aces, but there is still a cost penalty in terms of the recording medium – even removable hard drives cost more than tape in terms of the number of track-minutes each can hold. Hard disks can be archived to digital data tape systems, but this process is relatively slow. For a more thorough discussion of the implications of tapeless recording, refer to the chapter Hard Disk Recording.

Summary

Though few new analogue machines are now being built, I envisage them remaining popular for esoteric reasons in much the same way as tube processors and microphones are currently regarded. The well-equipped studio over the next few years will probably be able to offer a choice of analogue or digital multitracking and mastering as well as sophisticated hard disk-based recording and editing options. DAT remains the current 'standard' mastering format, but concerns over its reliability may eventually force the introduction of a truly professional alternative.

chapter 17

3D sound

Over the past couple of years, several devices which claim to create the illusion of three-dimensional sound from a standard two-speaker stereo system have come onto the market. The term 'three-dimensional' indicates that sounds in the mix can be made to appear to originate from a location outside the boundaries of the loudspeakers. Some processors, Roland's RSS (Roland Sound Space) processor in particular, are able, under certain circumstances, to create the illusion that the sound source actually moves behind the listener. Bearing in mind that all the sounds must emanate from two speakers in front of the listener, how is this possible?

3D Hearing

To understand how 3D sound systems work, it is necessary to know a little about how the human hearing system handles the directionality of sounds. Indeed, a little understanding of this subject helps us to position sounds in the normal stereo soundfield, so even if you have no intention of using a 3D processor, this section will be of value. Even so, I feel it's inevitable that low cost 3D sound processors will soon be a common feature of even small recording studios.

Just as our two eyes give us stereoscopic vision by presenting two simultaneous viewpoints of the world, our two ears do the same for sound. Only if a sound is directly ahead of us or directly behind us (or somewhere on an imaginary line joining the two points) do both ears register the same sound. The speed of sound being finite, it stands to reason that a sound originating directly from our right will arrive first at the right ear and then, some short time later, at the left ear. This time difference is noted by the brain and is just one of the means used to determine direction.

The sound arriving at the right ear will be unobstructed, while the sound arriving at the left ear will be masked by the head itself. This masking serves to reduce the level of the sound and also to modify its spectral content — high frequencies are attenuated more, whereas low frequencies remain relatively unaffected because their wavelength is significantly greater than the dimensions of the head. So far then, the human brain has three parameters to work on when analysing the input from a pair of ears: the time delay between the sound reaching first one and then the other ear; the difference in sound level occurring between the two ears; and the tonal change caused by the masking effect of the head. In contrast, a conventional pan pot only simulates one of these parameters: the level difference between the left and right ears.

Front Or Back?

Useful though the above explanation is, it doesn't tell us how we can discriminate between a sound that's directly in front of us or directly behind us, because in both cases, the signals arriving at both ears are identical. Similarly, if the sound originates at any point on the imaginary line drawn between these two extremes — such as directly over the head — the ears will still hear the same thing.

This is a more complex mechanism to comprehend, and it is thought that small, involuntary head movements help us to compare the signals arriving at both ears in the same way that we might move our head to establish visual parallax between two objects that are otherwise ambiguous. How important this mechanism is has not been confirmed, but there is another point to consider which is far easier to quantify. Ears are not just biological microphones stuck onto the side of the head, but are recessed and surrounded by the flaps of skin that we recognise as ears — more correctly termed 'pinnae'. This skin masks the inner ear from incoming sounds to a greater or lesser extent depending on the direction of the sound; measurements show that the effect of this masking is mainly spectral. In other words, the tonal property of the sound is changed in some way depending on its direction.

Dummy Head

When Roland developed their 3D sound system, they took the logical approach of using a dummy head, complete with pinnae, to analyse sounds originating at different positions around the head. The inter-aural level changes, time delays and spectral filtering effects were all noted and then used to control a set of computer-controlled filters, delays and level shifters which, in theory, would recreate the original sounds as perceived by a typical pair of ears. Indeed, they went further, making numerous measurements using volunteers with small microphones fitted into their ears to obtain a true average set of values.

The system so far, theoretically at any rate, allows a mono sound to be processed so that when monitored over good headphones, it can be positioned anywhere in front of, behind or above the listener using a couple of 360 degree pan pots, one for the horizontal plane and one for the vertical. However, such a system won't work effectively on loudspeakers, because when we listen to a conventional stereo system, some of the sound from the left speaker enters the right ear and vice versa. This crosstalk completely undermines the validity of the effect, so Roland went a stage further and measured this crosstalk in a typical listening room, then used the data to generate a crosstalk cancelling signal. In other words, what you shouldn't be hearing in the left ear (from the right speaker) is synthesized and then reversed in phase before being added to the normal left signal, and vice versa for the right. Now, if you're listening to a properly set up stereo system in a decent listening room from a point equidistant between the two speakers, it should be possible to perceive the processed sound coming from wherever the system positioned it.

There are an awful lot of 'ifs' in this explanation, and the fact is that none of the 3D sound systems works perfectly for all material or on all stereo set-ups. Most will enable sounds to be placed noticeably outside the speaker boundaries, and the result is very convincing, but any attempt to place the sound behind the listener depends for its success on several factors, including the kind of sound being processed. In practice, the illusion of sound coming from behind the listener tends to break down unless the sound is moving — if it is panned from one side at the front, round the back of the listener's head and then back to the front opposite side, the result can be very convincing indeed, but any attempt to place a stationary sound behind the listener tends to fail. To confuse matters, different listeners respond to these effects in different ways.

Consumer Systems

In recent years, a number of low cost stereo-in, stereo-out, spacial enhancement systems have appeared for use with computer games systems and home theatre. Though these fall short of convincing surround sound, they can widen the stereo image considerably, as well as adding to the feeling of spaciousness and depth.

The most effective models seem to work by exploiting the fact that the ear has a different frequency response depending on the angle of arrival of the sound, but as all stereo signals come from the same speakers, this effect is lost in conventional stereo reproduction. By adding tonal correction to the left and right components of the sound to simulate a sound being heard on axis, the perceived stereo image can be widened considerably without having to introduce the delays that normally cause mono compatibility problems. While these are unashamedly budget, domestic systems, the better ones can be useful in the studio, though because of the tonal changes they introduce, they're best used only on selected elements of the mix rather than on all of it. They work particularly well on effects returns, sound effects and extra percussion. Care must be taken with operating levels as most domestic products work at or around the -10dBv standard rather than +4dbu.

Mono Compatibility

While it would appear that all these systems offer a useful means of widening the available stereo image, and some can be used in a gimmicky way to move sounds or effects right around the listener's head, their real downfall is their lack of mono compatibility. This is inevitable, as real life can't be considered mono compatible, but as long as mono TV sound and mono radio receivers are with us, it has to be a cause for concern. The main problems are the phase and timbral changes that occur when the left and right signals are summed; the further the sound is panned by the 3D system outside the speakers, the more noticeable the side-effects become.

At the time of writing, more work is being done to improve the mono compatibility of these systems and to make their effects less dependent on the listener's position relative to the loudspeakers. Whether 3D systems will ever become fully effective is questionable at this stage, but the techniques that make these effects possible are already being employed in various pieces of studio equipment. Stereo sound samples are already being prepared via 3D sound systems, while the basic principles are being applied to widening the subjective sound of digital reverbs and other stereo effect processors.

Currently, 3D sound processors are expensive items and are limited in the number of channels that can be processed at any one time. However, their use requires no special skill, as the horizontal and vertical pan pots can be used quite intuitively, while the control movements (on some models) may be output as MIDI data and stored on a conventional MIDI sequencer, enabling some degree of automation. Whatever the limitations imposed by current processors of this type, their real beauty is that recordings need no decoding or special equipment at the user's end, and while, in its present state, 3D sound may be no substitute for true quadraphonic sound, it can be used

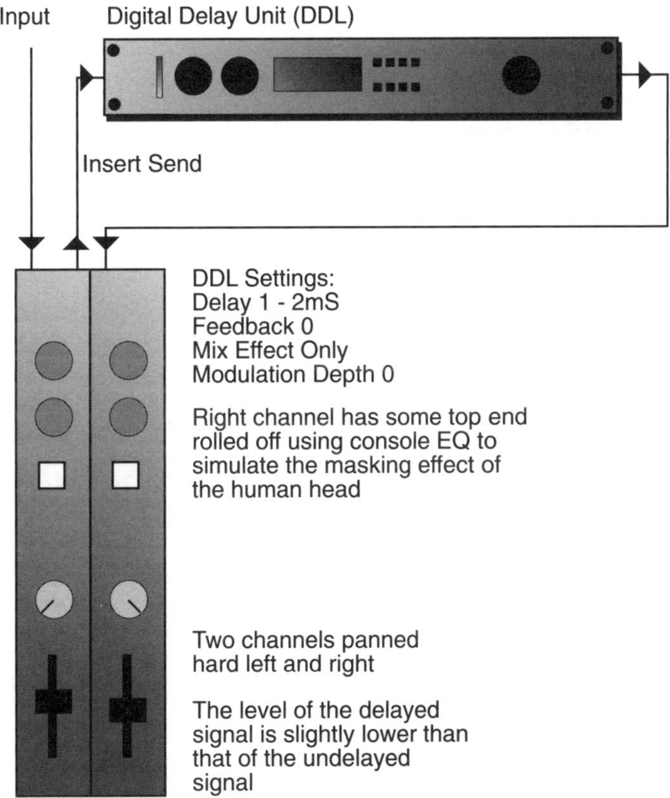
Input
Digital Delay Unit (DDL)
Insert Send
DDL Settings:
Delay 1 - 2mS
Feedback 0
Mix Effect Only
Modulation Depth 0
Right channel has some top end rolled off using console EQ to simulate the masking effect of the human head
Two channels panned hard left and right
The level of the delayed signal is slightly lower than that of the undelayed signal

Figure 17.1: Stereo Positioning using a DDL

to add interest to pop records and to enhance the special effects used in video movie soundtracks.

Stereo Effects

Having learned how the human hearing system perceives sound direction, it is possible to employ a little studio trickery to exploit these effects without having to buy special equipment. For example, we now know that to make a sound really appear as though it is coming from one side or the other, we not only have to change the relative left/right balance, but we also need to delay one of the signals slightly. The time taken for sound to travel around the human head is a little under 1mS, so it is useful to experiment with a DDL as shown in Figure 17.1. Here the signal is being panned to make it appear as though it is coming from the right hand side while a lower level, delayed version is panned to the left. This creates a more solid directional image than using the pan pot alone, though it isn't perfect because no account has been taken of the crosstalk between the speakers. The effect can be made slightly more authentic by rolling some of the top off the delayed signal to simulate the effect of head masking. The delayed signal only needs to be 3dB or so lower in level than the undelayed signal, and varying the delay time slightly varies the perceived sound location to some extent.

This principle is being unwittingly employed when a sound is split and a direct version of the sound panned to one extreme while a chorused or flanged version is panned to the other. The sense of depth and movement is due to the shifting delays between the processed signal and the unprocessed signal, making this a very powerful processing technique, even though the chorus/flanger need only be a mono unit. Variations on this effect are used extensively to enrich synthesized string and pad keyboard sounds or to create pseudo-stereo guitar chorus effects. These specific techniques are described in more depth in chapter 15.

chapter 18

headphones

Have you ever wondered why people don't just mix all their music on headphones? After all, it would reduce the amount of environmental noise considerably and would completely eliminate the need for acoustically treated control rooms. It sounds like the ideal solution, but unfortunately, headphones behave rather differently to loudspeakers in several key areas, and, as most music is optimised for loudspeaker playback, relying solely on headphones can be very misleading.

When stereophonic music is heard over a conventional pair of loudspeakers, our natural hearing mechanism positions the soundstage in front of us, whereas with headphones, there is little or no front-to-back information, which makes the sound appear to originate from either inside or above the listener's head. The problem of accurate stereo imaging is further compounded by the fact that when listening via loudspeakers (or, indeed, to a sound in real life) some of the sound from the left loudspeaker enters the right ear, and vice versa. With headphones, there is a very high degree of separation between the signals presented to the two ears, which produces an artificially enhanced sensation of stereo imaging. While this makes it difficult to predict the effect of the same musical mix over loudspeakers, it can be helpful in checking that all the sounds are where they were intended to be, and that any stereo effects sound properly balanced.

A more serious shortcoming of headphones is that different people will hear a different tonal balance, even though they are using the same model of headphone. This is particularly true at the low end of the audio spectrum, where factors such as the distance between the diaphragm and the ear and the effectiveness of the cushion seal will influence the amount of bass that the listener perceives. You can try this for yourself by listening via headphones and then pushing them closer to your ears; you should notice a dramatic increase in bass because the headphone diaphragm has moved closer to your ear and the proximity effect is causing a significant degree of bass lift.

The problem of maintaining an effective seal between the headphone and the area of head around the ear can be avoided by making the headphones acoustically open. In other words, instead of the headphone being in the form of a sealed enclosure which fits over the ears, the transducer is mounted in an acoustically transparent basket and spaced away from the head by means of padded cushions. Such open designs have the added advantage that the sound is less coloured than when confined by a sealed cavity, but the down side is that external sound is free to leak in and some of the sound from the headphones will leak out. This is not a problem when monitoring while mixing, but it can be troublesome when a performer is using such headphones to listen to a backing track or click track, as some of the spill from the headphones may leak back into the performer's microphone.

Though the sound quality of open headphones can be excellent and inconsistencies due to ineffective sealing can be largely eliminated, there is still some inconsistency in bass perception, caused by variation in the diaphragm/ear distance, which is dependent on the physical make-up of each individual ear. Where such headphones excel is in their ability to discriminate fine detail within a musical mix, and traces of distortion which can go unnoticed during loudspeaker listening are more likely to be picked up. Ideally, a mix should be checked on both headphones and loudspeakers, though for the home recordists working in a noise-sensitive environment, it is possible to do a considerable amount of work using headphones, resorting to loudspeakers only to check crucial stages of a mix for overall tonal balance.

chapter 19

mastering

One of the less glamorous but nevertheless essential tasks in any studio is to ensure that all tapes are properly labelled — to do otherwise risks at best confusion, and at worst, the erasure of an irreplaceable recording. There is now a standard tape labelling system put forward by the APRS (Association of Professional Recording Studios) which sets out to reduce the potential for error and which I shall describe briefly. This covers both multitrack and stereo master tapes, copies, clones and DAT. Colour coded labels are available via the APRS but simply writing the correct term on the box is a good start.

In all cases, tapes should be labelled with format details: in the case of analogue recordings, the tape speed, track format, noise reduction, EQ and, of course, the title and date of the recording are essential. Digital tapes should be labelled with sample rate and details of the type of machine used to make the recording. Open-reel tapes are traditionally stored 'tail out', as this reduces the degree of 'print-through' when the tapes are stored for a long time. The tapes must be rewound before playing.

Session Tape

The first tape created during a project is a Session Tape; this is usually a multitrack tape and comprises the first-generation recordings made during a session. In other words, it is the working tape on which material is recorded and overdubbed — consequently it may contain out-takes as well as wanted material. There may be several Session Tapes created during an album project. Session Tapes may be of any format and may be analogue or digital; indeed, in the case of direct-to-stereo recording, the original recording is still known as the Session Tape. All relevant data should be recorded on the tape box or inlay card. The APRS label is solid blue and bears the words SESSION TAPE.

Original Master

When a multitrack tape is first mixed to stereo, the result is the Original Master tape. It is the earliest generation of the final stereo recording. This is not necessarily the tape used for production, as it may later be necessary to add EQ or to edit the material. The APRS label is solid red with the legend ORIGINAL MASTER.

Production Master

The Production Master is usually an edited copy of the Original Master where the tracks have been placed in the correct running order and with correct spacing between the tracks. Often the Production Master will be equalised, and as different versions may be required for different release formats, the Production Master should be marked with the desired format: CD; Cassette; Vinyl; DCC or MiniDisk. The standard APRS label is solid green with the legend PRODUCTION MASTER. The label also includes space for release format details.

For digital formats such as CD, DCC or MiniDisk, the Production Master will have to be transferred to Sony U-Matic format at the mastering stage. Test tones should not be recorded onto tapes destined for digital formats. Many production masters are now made on DAT cassettes; a sampling rate of 44.1kHz is preferred if the machine allows it.

Production Master Copy/Clone

This is copied from the Production Master to allow distribution of the tape for manufacturing purposes without having to release the original Production Master. A tape copied in the analogue domain from either a digital or analogue source is known as a Copy while a digital clone of a digital original is known as a Clone. In theory, a clone will be identical to the original in all ways. The APRS label is bright orange with the words PRODUCTION MASTER COPY CLONE printed on it. The appropriate Copy or Clone box should be ticked and the label should include all information relating to the Production Master

Safety Copy Clone

This is strictly a backup copy or clone of another tape; the original from which it is taken should be clearly marked on the label. The label is bright pink and is legended SAFETY COPY CLONE. The appropriate Copy or Clone box should be ticked and the label should include all information relating to the original.

Not For Production

Description of any tape in any format which must not be used as a source for media manufacture. The label is yellow and bears the words NOT FOR PRODUCTION.

PQ Encoded Master Tape

This is the final U-Matic tape ready for the manufacture of a digital media release such as CD, DCC or MD and includes the coding information pertaining to number of tracks, playing time, table of contents and so on. Each of these release formats requires the PQ Encoded Master to be prepared in a specific way, so it is essential that the medium is identified on the label. The label is grey and is labelled PQ ENCODED TAPE MASTER. Tick boxes are provided for the various release media formats and whether the tape is an original or a clone.

Media Version

A copy or clone made for a specific purpose, such as radio broadcast or film/video soundtrack work. If the tape is recorded with timecode, this should be noted on the label. The label is yellow and marked MEDIA VERSION, with tick boxes for Radio, TV, Film or Video.

Tape Copying

When copying a tape, it is necessary to know the maximum recorded level on that tape. (This is not the case when making a digital clone, as the copy will be the same as the master tape in all respects.) Recordings are normally preceded by test tones, and the reference level of those tones should be marked on the tape box. Correctly recorded tones will be recorded with a burst in the left channel only at the start of the tones section, so it should be possible to check that you haven't got the right and left channels transposed. It is also wise to do a few spot checks throughout the tape to ensure that the test tones do in fact relate to the recorded level.

If the tape has been produced as a Production Master for CD (or other digital format) manufacture, there will be no test tones, in which case it may be necessary to play the material and establish at what level the peaks have been recorded.

Test Tones

The standard format for test tones is five seconds of 1kHz tone on the left channel only, followed by around 30 seconds of the same tone on both channels. The tone should be recorded at 0VU and the level noted on the box. It also helps alignment in the case of the tape being replayed on another machine if a 100Hz, 0VU tone is recorded, followed by a 10kHz tone, the latter often being recorded at around -10dB and the level again being noted.

In the case of digital tapes such as DAT, it is usual for them to be recorded so that the peak levels come to around 2dB below the maximum meter reading or FS (Full Scale). It is always a good idea to record a couple of minutes of silence onto the start of the tape, as the very start of a tape is more prone to errors. If continuous test tones are required for calibration, a nominal level of -14dBFS (1kHz) is considered acceptable and this should be noted on the label. At the end of the copy, there should be at least 30 seconds of recorded silence before the tape is stopped.

Record, Tape And CD Manufacture

With the advent of MiniDisk (MD) and Digital Compact Cassette (DCC), there are now five potential record release formats – and that doesn't include film or video soundtracks. The main formats at the time of writing remain compact disk (CD) and the analogue compact cassette, though vinyl is still a viable option, especially for specialist dance and club music.

The purpose of this chapter is to present an overview of the various processes that take place between completing a mix in the studio and the manufacture of a record from that recording.

Once the Session Tape (usually analogue or digital multitrack), has been mixed down to stereo, the resulting tape is designated the Original Master, and it is from this tape that a Production Master must be made. In all probability, the Original Master (or Masters) will contain out-takes, odd spuriae such as count-ins, and the material will probably be recorded in the wrong order with incorrect gap lengths between the songs. It may also be necessary to adjust the relative levels of some of the tracks and it is not uncommon to add further equalisation.

Working With DAT

When mixing to DAT, it is important to record as close as possible to the digital peak shown on the recorder's meters and to use the 44.1kHz sampling rate setting if available. When working with a DAT machine that has a fixed 48kHz sampling rate, don't worry – if you're planning to make CDs, the company who produce the CD Master tape for you should be able to handle this. However, never mix the two sample rates on one tape (or set of tapes) – you could end up with part of your album playing back at the wrong speed!

When making DAT Production Masters, always set start ID function to On. Normally, playing a song cued using an ID recorded with the Auto ID is to risk clipping the first note because Auto ID must sense the presence of the programme material before writing the ID. Because of this, it is wise to manually move all IDs back by half a second or so.

Avoid recording music on the first or last minute of tape and always record silence before and after the programme material – digital tapes contain sub-code information and it is important that this starts before the recording and continues for a while after it. Don't simply run the tape in play mode to create a gap as this will leave a section of tape with no sub-code.

Hard Disk Editing

While it is possible to make up a Production Master by compiling from one tape machine to another, a more precise option is to use a hard-disk editing system. These have the advantage that individual tracks can be 'topped and tailed' to ensure that they are clean up until the moment the first note sounds and that all count-ins and other unwanted material are removed. The edited material is then copied from the hard disk system to a stereo tape machine, ideally DAT, as the transfer can be made in the digital domain. This new tape is the Production Master. Digital formats such as DAT offer the advantage that the material can be cloned rather than copied making it possible to create backups and compiled Production Masters with no quality loss.

Production Master

When making the Production Master, a decision must be made as to whether the release will be on vinyl, cassette or disk. If it is to be on cassette, there must be a gap between the two sides and the playing times of the two sides must be calculated so as to be as equal as possible. As a rule, side one is made slightly longer than side two so that when the tape is turned over at the end of side one, side two is ready to play.

Careful listening is required to ascertain whether any of the tracks need adjusting in either level or EQ. The gaps between songs should also be auditioned, and though most are around four seconds, the actual length must be determined by ear; if the preceding song fades out, then a shorter gap may be required than if the song finishes abruptly. Essentially, if the gap feels right, it is right.

A full listing of the songs by title, start time (Start IDs) and playing time must accompany the Production Master and this sheet should include full details of the recording format such as sampling rate and, ideally, the type and model of machine that was used.

When compiling to open-reel analogue, the gaps are created by splicing either blank tape or leader tape between the songs. The length of blank tape required can be calculated from the running speed of the recorder.

The total time on a cassette can be a lot longer than on CD — most CDs offer a maximum recording time of 74 minutes. However, most commercial CDs are under 60 minutes in duration so this should present no problems. In the case of other formats, including vinyl, consult the manufacturer before producing the Production Master tape to find out the maximum playing time that can be accommodated.

What Comes Next

If you're planning to release your material only on analogue cassette, then a copy or clone of the Production Master may be all you need. Of course you also have to think about artwork, but that will be covered shortly.

Unfortunately the Production Master isn't the end of the line if you're aiming for a CD release — there are two more stages to negotiate: the CD Master tape and the Glass Master. Similarly, if you're going to add either MiniDisk or DCC to your release formats, you'll need to speak to the manufacturers as to their requirements. At the time of writing, these formats are still very new, so direct contact with the manufacturers is recommended. The main difference between MD and DCC and the established formats is that both newcomers use a form of data compression to reduce the amount of digital data to around one fifth of that of a conventional CD or DAT tape. Furthermore, both formats have the ability to store text, which can be used to display such things as the song titles on those machines equipped with display windows.

CD Mastering

For CD mastering, the Production Master tape will be arranged with no gap between the two sides of the album and a total playing time, including gaps, of less than 74 minutes. The factory will require a fully prepared CD Master tape, which is most often handled by a specialist mastering facility and involves cloning or copying the Production Master to a U-Matic Tape. This is PCM encoded, timecoded and has the necessary PQ (Pause and Cue) code information added. This information is used to create the Table of Contents (or TOC) on the finished CD so that a CD player can locate the tracks. A track title and time sheet will also be produced at this time for use by the CD manufacturers, usually by the company that produces the CD Master tape.

Some mastering facilities can make a Reference CD from the CD Tape Master. This is relatively inexpensive, and the small outlay is worth it for the peace of mind in knowing that the finished product will turn out as you expected it. If a proper reference CD is unavailable, a one-off CDR disk is better than nothing, though the track start times may not accurately reflect those on the finished product.

While on the subject, the falling cost of low-volume CDR duplication may eventually make this a viable alternative to conventional manufacture for small quantity runs of 50 disks or less. These may be made directly from a Production Master tape, saving the cost of having a CD Master tape produced.

Glass Masters

At the CD plant, the CD Tape Master has to be played into a Glass Mastering Machine which uses all the special coding on the tape to determine timing and Table of Contents. After the data has been transferred to the Glass Master (so called because a glass disk is used to carry the photosensitive surface which is imprinted with digital data from a modulated laser), the Glass Master is plated with nickel to make a mechanical stamper, similar in concept to that used to stamp out vinyl records.

During manufacture, the reflective part of the CD is stamped out of aluminium and then sandwiched between layers of transparent plastic which protect it and give it rigidity. Labels are printed directly onto the pressed CD using a special, quick-drying ink, and may be in single or multiple colours. The manufacturer should be consulted as to what form the original artwork should take.

After manufacture, the discs are automatically loaded into jewel cases along with an inlay card and booklet. These must be provided by the client prior to manufacture. Few CD pressing plants handle their own inlay card printing, but most will be able to recommend a company that can do this for you or arrange printing on your behalf. However, if you don't arrange the printing yourself, there are going to be at least two other businesses in the chain which increases the possibility of error.

Brokers

An alternative approach to CD production is to negotiate a package price with a broker who will handle all the aspects of record or CD production, including the various mastering stages, printing and packaging. However, don't assume that everything will proceed smoothly — check at every stage if at all possible. Also check at the outset that there are no hidden costs; companies quoting attractive prices for CD manufacture often don't include essential services such as producing the CD Master Tape, Glass Mastering and printed material — these are all priced as extras. Realistically, a minimum practical production run of CDs is 500, with 1,000 or more being even more cost effective.

Try to find a Broker recommended by someone you know if at all possible because, as in all areas of business, there is a vast difference in quality between the best and worst companies offering what is ostensibly the same service.

Vinyl

Vinyl records are produced using metal stampers which, in turn, start life as a pair of Lacquer Masters, one for each side of the record. These are cut from blanks using a record cutting lathe and then taken to the record manufacturing plant where the stampers are made. The stampers (or Factory Masters) are formed onto the lacquers using an electro-plating process.

The actual record labels are printed on paper using special heat-resistant inks; most record plants have the facility to arrange manufacture. Fixing of the labels is achieved during the pressing process, and once the records have been trimmed of waste material and inspected, they are placed in sleeves. Inner sleeves are often optional, so discuss sleeve requirements with the factory when discussing cost. As with CDs, the minimum practical quantity for manufacture is several hundred.

Compact Cassette

High Speed Copying

Cassettes may be made from a Production Master tape, ideally in DAT format. In the case of high speed copying, the Production Master will normally be copied onto a special analogue machine designed to work at high speed. The recording is made onto cassette tape stored on large reels (or 'pancakes'), which is wound into empty cassette shells after recording. This procedure offers the advantage that the tape can be cut exactly to length, and the copying process is not compromised by the mechanics of the cassette shells.

As a rule, both sides of the tape are copied at the same time, and unless you state otherwise, the recordings will be made using Dolby B noise reduction. Depending on your budget, there is a choice of standard Fe tape or Type II tape, also known as Chrome equivalent. Standard cassette shells are available in black or white.

Solid-state memory stores have replaced high speed tape for mastering purposes in some duplicating plants, and in theory, these produce less degradation in audio quality. Essentially the whole album is loaded into a large digital memory in real time and then clocked out at the high speed during the copying process.

Real Time Copying

Real time copies may be made directly from a DAT source; the destination cassettes are usually pre-loaded with tape. This gives less flexibility as regards playing time, but has the advantage that low production runs are economically viable.

High Speed Cassette To Cassette Copying

The least satisfactory method of cassette duplication is the high speed system which works from a cassette master and records onto pre-loaded blank cassettes. The tape guides in cassette shells don't work well at high speeds, which leads to inconsistent recording quality. The fact that the Production Master must be copied to cassette also introduces another generation of quality loss into the duplication process.

Labelling

Cassettes may use printed paper labels or the printing may be done directly onto the cassette shell. This latter process must be done during the duplication process and is only cost effective for runs of several hundred tapes or more due to the cost of making the special printing plates. As a rule, paper labels give more scope in the use of colour and design.

Packaging

Cassettes are normally delivered in transparent library boxes and the folded inlay cards are generally printed separately. For small runs, these may be inserted by hand. In the case of very small runs, it may be worth using a colour photocopy bureau to copy the original artwork.